Pencil Sketch by Barrie Waugh

CONTENTS

Goodbye to Elvis. 7
Elvis Personal Album. 10
The Louisiana Hayride. 12
1956. 18
Aloha From Hawaii. 32
Graceland 34
My Las Vegas. 44
How I Met Elvis. 50
Elvis Personal Album. 52
The Jackie Gleason Show. 58
Old Shep. 60
King of Rock'n'Roll?. 64
The Colonel's Story. 66
Elvis' Sun Career. 76
Elvis Personal Album. 82
Play It James!. 86
Elvis Island Discs. 90

That Loved-on Look. 94
Two British Rarities. 94
Is Criticism of Movies Justified?. 97
The World's Greatest Showman. 106
The Man Behind the Music. 114
Elvis Said. 120
History of LP Cover. 130
Sole Possession of the King. 146
One Step Further. 148
The Elvis Presley Story. 161
The MGM Story. 172
Elvis Country. 180
Full list of Elvis films. 190
List of the King's singles. 191

Some of the articles in this compendium
were written before the untimely death
of The King in August 1977.

THE MAN AND HIS MUSIC

GOODBYE TO ELVIS

Elvis Presley died on August 16th, at Graceland, his Memphis home.

Immediately the news was announced, fans the world over went into mourning. Some broke down in tears, as if at the loss of a close friend, while for others it was a time for quiet reflection, on a favourite song, or a film role, or perhaps even a touching moment in the personal life of this unique man.

How can we best say goodbye to Elvis? This book is our tribute to him, but words cannot express the love and devotion felt by his loyal fans. Elvis is The King – perhaps that simple phrase says enough.

Elvis lay in state in the hallway of Graceland, while fans from all over America and beyond waited quietly outside the white iron gates to pay their last respects. The line was fifteen deep and stretched for half a mile.

Then came the day of the funeral, on August 18th. A private service was held at Graceland, attended by close family and friends, before at last the 27-car cortege left the mansion on its way to Forest Hills Cemetery. Police who were expecting that the crowd would surge forward at the first sign of the cream Cadillac hearse need not have worried. There was hardly a movement in the respectful and grieving crowd.

All the flags in Tennessee had been lowered to half mast, and wreaths and bouquets had been flown in from all over the world. The four-mile drive to the cemetery was lined with mourners of every age, creed and colour.

At the cemetery there was a brief service by Elvis' favourite clergyman, the Rev. C. W. Bradley, of the Church of Christ. Then Elvis was laid to rest in a mausoleum, close to his mother. The mausoleum will now become a shrine for admirers to visit.

Hours after the ceremony, thousands of people lingered outside the cemetery gates, and thousands more stood silently outside the walls of Graceland.

The world will always remember Elvis.

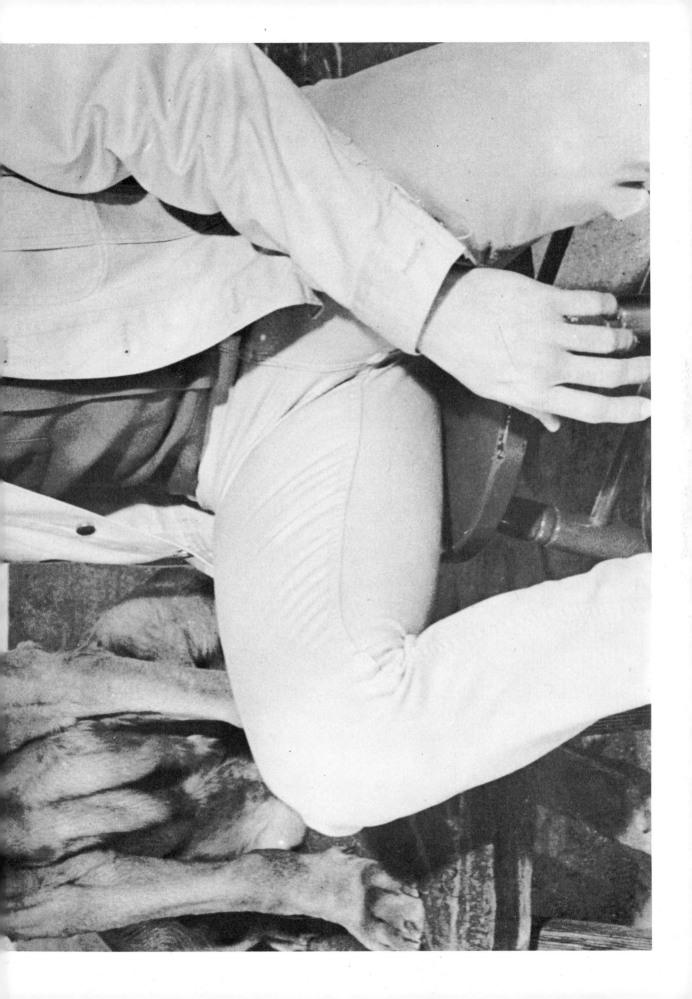

ELVIS PERSONAL ALBUM

Top left: *At the back of* "Graceland".
Left: *Relaxing at* "Graceland".
Below: *At Audobon Drive.*

Early Shots 1956-8

Top left: *With fans during the festive season.*

Bottom left: *Again with fans, this time at Audobon Drive.*

Below: *Signing autographs at the "Graceland Gates".*

The LOUISIANA HAYRIDE

★

—The Trip to Stardom

by Vee Gee

The month was October, in the year of 1954. This was the birth of Elvis Presley as far as many people were concerned, for it was the memorable occasion when Elvis appeared on radio for the very first time. The nickname for the show was "The cradle of stars" and they weren't far wrong, for the "Louisiana Hayride" was responsible for more people reaching fame and fortune from near obscurity than any other show broadcast over the United States.

"Hayride" began its journey in April of 1948, and even today, although it doesn't have regular times of showing, it still has occasional shows which bring back happy memories of the immortal Hank Williams, never-to-be-forgotten Jim Reeves and one unheard-of Elvis Presley. As a weekly programme it ceased to operate after 1957, and if at that time people didn't think it a small tragedy that the show had wound up, then they are beginning to realize now just how much they have to thank the programme for – and

especially the programme director, Mr Frank Page.

The very first show was put out on April 3, 1948 and it was a real live talent show operating from Shreveport, Louisiana every Saturday night. It was a few months after this opening night that Hank Williams made his first appearance. The exact date was August 7, and he left the show on June 3, 1949, a national star. He promised to return to the show some day, and he did – on September 4, 1952, and he was signed on a lengthy contract. Everyone knows the story from then on. Approximately thirteen weeks later he died leaving behind him a legend that

will live as long as folk music and country and western itself.

Jim Reeves was "discovered" by "Louisiana Hayride" working as a D.J. for a radio station at Hendersonville, Texas. Incidentally, after becoming a big star Jim bought this station himself. Nearly all Jim's first big hits were recorded at the KWKH studios, where "Hayride" was broadcast from.

Slim "Rosemarie" Whitman was also discovered on this show, and it was he who tipped them off about Elvis Presley. It appears that in between his "Hayride" appearances, Slim had done a show in Memphis, Tennessee. He came to

Louisiana full of talk about a kid ("some funny name I can't remember") who he was convinced would be a gas on "Hayride". He put Elvis on the same show as himself and even Slim had to admit that Elvis stole it from him.

Not long afterwards a record on the "Sun" label caused a real commotion in the studio, for someone had brought them an Elvis record (believed to be "That's Alright Mama"). After hearing it, Page got on the phone to Sam Phillips, in Memphis, who, as everyone knows, was the head of "Sun" records, and in a matter of minutes Elvis was booked for the show – October, 1954. He proved to be a sensation and came back a second time. It was then that he was signed on a year's contract.

At that time he was backed by Scotty Moore and Bill Black. For each show Scotty and Bill received a sum of twelve dollars, and Elvis, eighteen dollars. This amount seems almost unbelievable, but it only cost adults some sixty cents (3s. 6d.) and children thirty cents to see it.

Elvis worked for a whole year under this contract, and used to drive down from Memphis every Saturday evening. It was during this time that his backing group, Scotty and Bill were joined by drummer D. J. Fontana, who said of Elvis: "It's a real pleasure for me to work with him. He knows what he wants and goes out to get it, though he never wastes time on a session. He's a great feller."

After the first six months of his contract, Elvis found that he couldn't possibly fit "Hayride" any longer into his weekly schedule, which was already so tightly packed it tended to overflow at the top! Regrettably, he was forced to step down, and at the same time pay a four hundred dollar bill each and every time he should have appeared and didn't.

It was with the money from the first of his shows on "Louisiana Hayride" that he bought his mother a car – even before he could afford one for himself, and I am sure when Elvis thinks back to these early "Hay-days" he must feel a touch of nostalgia as I do when I look back at photos of Elvis, taken more than a decade ago, wearing a shocking pink suit and chrome shoes, belting out one of his early rockers. Somehow there was more excitement attached to everything in those days.

1956

by TONY NEALE

Sometime during 1956, RCA-Victor decided to set up a photo-session for their premier artiste; so Elvis picked up his guitar, donned a candy-striped shirt and flaming-red sports jacket, gave that slick greasy hair an extra comb, and duly obliged. One result of this session can be found gracing the covers of two sadly deleted British EPs: "Elvis Presley (I Need You So)", and "Strictly Elvis"; but the most imposing shot is the one featured on the second Presley LP: "Elvis" (titled "Rock 'n' Roll, No. 2" in Britain), and this is the subject of the following article.

That cover-shot on the second album is one of the finest ever featured on a Presley collection, with the young Elvis captured in a perfect profile study, strumming a guitar and gazing wistfully up towards some elusive, hypnotic star in the musical sky; a fifties rock 'n' roll hybrid, borrowing from Jimmie Rodgers, Hank Williams and every Southern country boy who ever picked up a battered old guitar and sang away his joys and sorrows. And, as if this wasn't enough, the record also carried easily the most intelligent sleeve-notes found on a Presley album, spotlighting the various sources from which Elvis borrowed to create that unique, "untouchable" sound; from the gospel of the Blackwood Brothers and Mahalia Jackson, to the more sophisticated styles of Bill Kenney and the Ink Spots and "Ivory" Joe Hunter.

It's interesting to note here that, for some strange reason, the British cover of this LP issued on HMV was completely different to the Stateside release; instead we got a picture of Elvis taken (I believe) backstage at one of the Tupelo concerts in late '56, leering at the camera under heavy-lidded eyes, with a vivid yellow background artificially superimposed. This cover is perhaps typical of many fifties' album sleeves, being the personification of bad taste and yet, nonetheless, very effective and totally right for the raw, uninhibited music that was rock 'n' roll: just as priceless in its own way as the American cover.

I reckon the second Presley album is the most significant collection, if not of his whole career, then certainly as regards pre-Army material, and for these reasons: Elvis' first LP was without doubt a stunning collection of high-octane tracks all of which remain classics to this day; but, good as it was, that initial set was as much a compilation album as anything else, consisting of seven early Victor sides and five older Sun out-takes which, great as they are, were never really intended for release. Although if Sun had ever gotten around to issuing a Presley album, no doubt several of these unissued cuts would have ended up on it.

In contrast, the second album was the first example of Elvis going into the studio specifically to produce an LP; a few of the numbers on the first album, such as "Lawdy Miss Clawdy", did reflect the then current Presley style; but tracks like "I Love You Because" were already almost two years old and didn't really represent the Presley '56 sound. The second LP, with all the tracks bar one recorded between 1–3 September '56? The second LP provides the answer, so let's when the record was issued shortly afterwards; representing the fifties Elvis more faithfully than any other, neither bowing to the commercialism of the soundtrack albums, nor the limitations of the first Christmas collection. Discounting seasonal and movie material, it was the only really representative Presley set to be issued until 1960 and: "Elvis Is Back".

So just where was Elvis at, musically, in late '56? The second LP provides the answer so let's take it gently to pieces and try not to let nostalgia get in the way too often.

A rough breakdown of the album runs something like this: three unashamed rockers, four ballads, a couple of blues, one pop item and two outright country numbers. So, even though all the material, except one track, was recorded at the same time, there is a variety of styles featured, demonstrating that despite the "King of rock" tag, Elvis has always been much more than that; something which his fans knew all along, but which took his detractors a lot longer to realise, or admit.

Looking at the rockers first, it's interesting to

note that all three of them were big hits for Little Richard; obviously a favourite Presley artist. Richard's songs tended to be pretty similar in construction, giving these upbeat tracks a samey flavour, although Elvis still managed to give each song an individual treatment. The only previous Richard number which Elvis had attempted was "Tutti Frutti", cut back at the 31 January '56 session, along with "Gonna Sit Right Down And Cry"; it's interesting to compare the earlier track with the later efforts, showing that the Presley sound, however gradually, was beginning to lose those rough edges, giving way to a still exciting but, nonetheless, slightly more stylised sound. The earlier cut seems to have just a shade more energy, being taken at the usual frantic Presley pace, but there's not a lot you can do with a song which is virtually an endless repetition of the title and, for me, the highlight of "Tutti Frutti" is Scotty Moore's typically aggressive guitar break. The later Richard tracks still manage to whip up a lot of excitement but the edge of the earlier cut is all but gone, although "Ready Teddy" is still, to my mind, the most exciting of the whole bunch. I admit, though, that I've been influenced by seeing the Ed Sullivan TV performance of this number by Elvis on the "On Tour" movie. Apart from this though, "Ready Teddy" really swings, pounding along with manic abandon and featuring some brilliant drumming from D. J. Fontana.

The thing I always dug about "Long Tall Sally" and "Rip It Up" was the way Elvis' thick southern accent featured strongly throughout the songs; listen during "Rip It Up" to the line beginning: "Long about ten I'll be flyin' high", you could cut the accent with a knife. I think that these individual tracks would have made even more impact if they'd been issued on different

records, rather than bunched together as they are on the second LP. It would have been nice to see a Presley version of Joe Turner's "Flip, Flop And Fly" on the album since it was one of Elvis' favourites, but we got "Shake, Rattle And Roll" so I'm not complaining!

Regarding the ballad tracks, well I always think of them in terms of three good and one indifferent; let's take the two most well-known numbers first.

"Love Me" was the most popular song Stateside, selling a million after its inclusion on an EP which also featured "Rip It Up", "When My Blue Moon Turns To Gold" and "Paralysed"; no doubt the song's exposure on the Sullivan TV show also boosted the record's phenomenal US sales. Fats Domino had the original version, but Presley's is the definitive one; acres of heavy breathing and mangled-phrasing had the female fans buying it in droves (Elvis really teased the audience during the Sullivan show while performing this number, leaving heavily on the low notes and deliberately messing around with the words). Jerry Leiber and Mike Stoller, who wrote the song were reportedly less than enthused with their creation, and I reckon Elvis gives them a better treatment of it than they had any right to expect. "Love Me" may have been the *numero uno* track in the States, but here in Britain "Old Shep" was the one which had the tears flowing and the handkerchiefs dabbing away, recounting as it did the maudlin tale of a boy and his faithful dog; a standard country weeper which Elvis had performed as a child in an amateur talent contest. When I first obtained the "Rock 'n' Roll, No. 2" LP in the early sixties I was more interested in rock and tended to skip over this lengthy ballad in the rush to get to "Ready Teddy", but over the years my admiration for the Presley performance

20

on this track has increased with every playing. The subject is very mawkish and, sung by a lesser artist, could easily have degenerated into cloying sentimentality; but Elvis' vocal is really superb: clear, precise and always in complete control.

Anyone who can sing the line: "Old Shep he has gone where the good doggies go" without provoking instant laughter must have something going for him, and Elvis pulls it off without even trying.

Apart from any musical considerations, "Old Shep" is also notable for being the only track I can recall which RCA have issued by mistake, shoving out the wrong "take" on a few copies of the second LP. Apparently, on the 1960 pressing of the album, RCA included an alternate version of the number, cut at the same session as the common version; and, since copies containing this cut are limited, it makes it possibly the rarest Presley item on record, barring unissued Sun sides. I've been kicking myself for the last decade because I actually had a copy containing the rare version and very cleverly managed to lose it some years back! For any sceptics who might be reading this, I can assure them the alternate take definitely exists, but the only way to get hold of it is to check any US copies of the album which feature the original RCA black label; you might strike lucky but beware, both versions are very similar, which is no doubt why the mistake happened in the first place. In a nutshell, the rare version has slightly more bluesy guitar touches, and on the vocal of the common version Elvis sings "His eyes were fast growing dim", whereas on the alternate take he includes the word "And" at the beginning of that line. No doubt there's other subtle differences but my memory's a bit dodgy after all these years; anyhow, if anyone out there has a copy with the rare "Old Shep" I wish they'd let me know about it!

The third class "A" ballad is "How's The World Treating You", otherwise known as "instant depression"; if you're feeling suicidal at all, this track will push you over the edge without any trouble. My sentiments regarding this song are similar to "Old Shep", it would be easy to overdo the pathos but Elvis' beautiful vocal coupled with restrained but, nonetheless, effective guitar and piano combine to make it one of his finest-ever ballad sides.

Now we come to, not only the one bad ballad on this LP, but, in my opinion, the only duff track on the whole record. Not since "Blue Moon" has so much echo been unloaded onto an unsuspecting singer, as on "First In Line"; it sounds like Elvis is singing through a megaphone

at the bottom of a forty-foot well, the echo really seems to hang over the number like an impenetrable fog. The song itself is strange enough to begin with, being roughly in the style of say, "I Was The One", but really seeming to exist in a world of its own; perhaps the nearest to it in style is "I Want You, I Need You". To be fair to Elvis, I reckon he does what he can with the song, but he's fighting half a ton of echo and a mediocre composition so it's no fair contest. Despite what I've said about it, though, this track still has a weird, surreal charm all its own, although I still wish Elvis had shelved it in favour of something a little more worthy of his talents—like maybe "Flip, Flop And Fly"! There's only one track on this LP that could be labelled straight "pop" and that's "Paralysed"; after the runaway success of "Don't Be Cruel", Elvis was naturally on the lookout for a similar biggie from the same writer, and certainly this Otis Blackwell number is an ideal vehicle for the Presley style. Tracks such as this and "Don't Be Cruel" anticipated the more commercialised pop/rock sound of the '57 Elvis, featured on numbers like "All Shook Up" and "Treat Me Nice"; and it's no surprise that "Paralysed" scored well when issued as a single in Britain, reaching the no. 8 position in the *New Musical Express* top 30; a strong, commercial number with a cheerful, infectious quality. Another point of interest about this track is that it's spliced from at least two different takes, a fact which I only noticed recently; the sound on the very last line: "All I could do was stand there Paralysed", is different from the rest of the song, with a touch more treble giving a tinnier quality. Some clumsy production work there!

It's fair to say that Elvis' country origins hover • over the whole of his second LP but there are only two out-and-out country tracks included on it; the first of these: "When My Blue Moon Turns To Gold Again", is my favourite of the two and one of the best cuts on the album. This beautiful number showcases, perhaps more than any other song, the genuine depth and richness of the Presley voice. The key is somewhat lower than you might expect from Elvis and, what with the sleepy melody and typical slurring of words from Elvis, the track has a vaguely hypnotic effect. The song seems to be a particular favourite of Elvis' because he featured the number on the 6 January '57 edition of the Ed Sullivan Show. Before singing the song, Elvis thanked the audience for their support and told them he'd received "exactly 282 Teddy-bears" during the Christmas holidays, adding that he'd "wanted to buy all the fans a new Lincoln but they won't let

me"! The Sullivan version of the song was drowned somewhat by much screaming but you can still hear Scotty's guitar rolling out some nice runs in the background. Speaking of Scotty, I reckon his solo on this number is one of the best he ever did; it's typically Scotty in that, although the break is basically country in construction, he manages to inject a shot of blues in their somewhere. What a guitarist this man is! I could discuss his playing for hours. I must say I have one reservation about "When My Blue Moon", and that concerns the ending; I think the dramatic, drawn-out finish is a bit out of place and should have been shelved in favour of a more modest finale, in keeping with the general mood of the song. However, if they'd stuck a trombone solo at the end, both the Presley vocal and Scotty's picking would have more than compensated for it.

Rounding off the LP on side two is the second country item: "How Do You Think I Feel", a throwback to the earlier Presley style; very similar, in fact, to certain Sun sides (notably: "You're A Heartbreaker" and "I Don't Care If The Sun Don't Shine"). This somewhat eccentric track steams along at a brisk canter with what sounds like somebody plucking a giant rubber-band in the background. I don't think Elvis enjoyed being described as a "Hillbilly" singer in the early days, but it would be hard to come up with a better description of this particular number; as you listen to it you can almost see the ancient model "T" Ford stuck firmly in the mud beside the chicken-run, and the illicit still steaming away on the back-porch.

The strange thing about this track is that although the lyrics are about unrequited love, the general mood of the song is so jolly it takes you a while to realise this fact: "How do you think I feel?" asks a petulant Elvis, and the girl could be forgiven for replying: "Happy as a sandboy," judging by the lively vocal! This is probably a number which Elvis would have got around to cutting for Sun, had he remained with that label; but this late '56 side shows that, even while singing basic country material, the Presley sound was gradually changing, with the vocals and backing becoming just that bit more stylised. "How Do You Think I Feel" is very much in the style of those Sun classics, but somehow you just know it couldn't be a Sun recording, the naievety has diminished in favour of a more driving, aggressive approach; it's listening to tracks like this that makes me wonder just what numbers Elvis would have cut had he stayed with Sun records.

Only two tracks to go on Elvis' second album, and it's blues all the way; let's consider the most obscure number first: "Anyplace Is Paradise" is one of those enigmatic tracks peppered about several of the early Presley albums, along with things like: "Gonna Sit Right Down And Cry", and "One-sided Love Affair"; numbers which rarely seem to crop up during discussions about the Presley career, but which remain classics of their kind.

"Paradise" is a deliciously relaxed blues item which these days would probably be called "laid-back"; I know Elvis has many sides but I maintain he's never better than when tackling a lazy, raunchy number such as this. The track has a very spaced-out, after-hours feel to it, with some restrained but oh so effective piano and guitar, lending great atmosphere to the whole thing. I'd like to know where Elvis got hold of this song, and who the writer, Joe Thomas, is; I vaguely remember seeing his name while sorting through a pile of fifties "doo-wop" albums in a rock 'n' roll oldies shop, but apart from that I know nothing about him or the history of the song. It's always been my dream that Elvis would do a whole album of this sort of material, but I guess it'll never happen now. "Anyplace Is Paradise" remains one of my favourite Presley sides and one which I reckon has never commanded the attention it obviously deserves.

I've purposely left my own favourite track on the "Elvis" album until last; the most overlooked of the three Arthur Crudup songs cut by Elvis, but every bit as good as the other two. It also happens that "So Glad You're Mine" is the one track on this second LP which wasn't recorded along with the other songs in September '56, coming instead from the 30 January '56 session which also produced "One-sided Love Affair", "Blue Suede Shoes" and another Crudup classic, "My Baby Left Me".

When I first bought this second Elvis LP, apart from the odd track or two, all the material was new to me, and I remember that when I put on side two of the record, "So Glad You're Mine" really wiped me completely out; the whole sound seemed that much more aggressive and committed, and for sheer excitement it towered over the other tracks. At that time I knew nothing about it being an earlier recording but I knew it sounded different somehow; nowadays, after many playings, the track seems to fit in more easily with the later material on the album, but I've never forgotten the feeling it gave me the first time I heard it. I've always thought of this track as a much heavier version of "Anyplace Is

Paradise" since they're similar kinds of song, yet both are different enough in approach to stand up independently.

Right from Shorty Long's raunchy piano intro, through one of Scotty's finest guitar-breaks (just listen to that tough sound!), and Elvis' impassioned vocal, this is all the way along one of Elvis' greatest recordings; it knocks the Crudup original into next week. One thing that puzzles me about "So Glad You're Mine" is why it wasn't included on the first Presley LP; RCA even used some unissued Sun material to make up the tracks for the initial album, and yet they left this freshly recorded track until the second collection. The only reason I can think of is that just before Scotty's solo you can hear a strange little squeak, like a rusty hinge; what it is I don't know, I used to puzzle for hours over it, playing the track over and over again, but I'm none the wiser today. Anyway, it may be this slight fault that decided RCA against putting it out; seems a small reason but I can't think of any other.

Thank God they didn't leave the song in the vaults because it really is a superb example of Elvis at his artistic peak, on the sort of material he performs so well; it's tracks like this one plus "Lawdy Miss Clawdy" and "Mystery Train" which earned Elvis the richly deserved title of finest white rhythm and blues singer ever. I don't say he still is, but in those days nobody could come near him on this kind of number.

So that's the "Elvis, Rock 'n' Roll, No. 2" album, an excellent set by virtue of the musical content but also, as I said earlier, significant in that it's arguably his most representative fifties collection. (I won't argue with those fans who disagree in favour of the first Presley LP; track for track, that record is probably better, especially the British version which featured different tracks than the US one, but the second album reflected the then contemporary Presley style more faithfully than any other fifties set, in my opinion.) After this LP came a succession of seasonal and movie soundtrack LPs, unbroken until 1960 and the "Elvis Is Back" set, with a handful of classic non-movie singles in between, allowing the natural Presley style to shine through now and again. I'm sorry that there was never a "Rock 'n' Roll, No. 3" from Elvis but I shouldn't be greedy; after all the material on volumes 1 and 2 will stand forever, and forever is a long, long time.

TONY NEALE

ELVIS —
Aloha from Hawaii

by DAVID TROTTER

At 12.30 a.m. Hawaiian time, January 14th 1973, morse code zipped across millions of T.V. screens all over the world spelling out, "Elvis Presley, Aloha From Hawaii Via Satellite". This "live" Rock-concert was to be proved the greatest ever Elvis show. To start the Special a film of Elvis arriving in Hawaii, clad in a white corduroy suit, red shirt, and many Hawaiian garlands. He walks the aisle to the Honolulu International Center Arena shaking hands, and collecting more leis on his way, acknowledging many fans who have lined the sidewalks. "Aloha From Hawaii" was to be the biggest and first Rock concert to be relayed to such a vast audience of 1.5 billion people throughout the world. Elvis said in a short press conference held when the Satellite special plans became final:

"It's very hard to comprehend. In fifteen years it's very hard to comprehend this happening."

The reason for the show was that Elvis had always been in great demand for "live" appearances in many countries around the world and it was agreed that this was the best way for the King's worldwide fans to get a chance to see him perform "live" at the actual time of the concert being performed. The proceeds of the show were donated to a cancer fund set up in memory of Kui Lee, one of Hawaii's leading composers. The initial target was to raise 25,000 dollars, but the response was so great that the final total reached 75,000 dollars. A total of 6,000 tickets were sold strictly by donation but care was taken that poorer fans were not left out in the cold. Tickets ranged from 80 cents to 1,000 dollars.

The show itself was dynamite. Thunderous and hysteric applause heralded Elvis' entrance with the King gathering Hawaiian leis from the fans on his way to centre stage. Resplendent in a white jumpsuit and matching cape displaying a huge U.S.A. dollar eagle sparkling in the coloured lights and innumerable flashes as cheers rose from El's opening number, "CC Rider". Rainbow-coloured spotlights and neon flashes spelling out Elvis' much-loved name popped on and off constantly in the background. "Burning Love" brought great applause from the fans, followed by Elvis' opening and welcome speech.

"We hope you enjoy our show tonight. We're gonna try and do all the songs you wanna hear."
Screams bring forth a new song, "Something". A George Harrison composition which proved a firm favourite with the crowd. There wasn't a dry eye after "You Gave Me A Mountain", with viewers been given an extra treat by seeing sometimes 4 multiple Elvis pictures on the screen at the same time. "Steam Roller Blues" came next and there was plenty of fooling around during this number. Front row females burning in their element.

"My Way" was very good and sung with much sincerity. A medley of the King's records followed, including "Blue Suede Shoes", "Johnny B. Goode", "Love Me" etc. Elvis then sings the saddest song he's ever heard. "I'm So Lonesome I Could Cry", with Elvis' voice trembling lovingly on the sad endings to each verse. Marvellous! "live" show favourites such as "I Can't Stop Loving You" and "Hound Dog" followed, being shorter versions of both songs. Fabulous close-ups during "What Now My Love" and extra karate kicks, shaking of legs, and thrusting forward during "Fever". A despatch of 3 scarves blue, white, and pink, during "Welcome To My World" and more karate showmanship during the Vegas smash number "Suspicious Minds". "I'll Remember You" gaining terrific applause and sung beautifully. Rock medley, "Long Tall Sally" and "Whole Lotta Shakin' Goin' On" works the audience to fever pitch, only to be cooled down with a terrific patriotic rendering of "An American Trilogy" bringing a one minute ovation at the end of the song. Rock numbers "Big Hunk O' Love" followed and then the end of the show and "Can't Help Falling In Love". Perhaps more nostalgic here more than anywhere else as the song did originate from the movie "Blue Hawaii". As the drum-rolls pound out the closing vamp, Elvis walks along the catwalk shaking hands with the audience and reaching out to fans. The King is given a gold crown from a front row admirer and throws his cape into the audience.

As they say, all good things come to an end! The concert was fabulous, the album was dynamite, and the man himself, fantastic!

It is an experience to say the least to see the show in its entirety. The smash-gold-award "Aloha From Hawaii" album was released to mark the greatest Rock-concert ever, and mark it it did.

"Aloha From Hawaii" now stands in the highest rank ever. The greatest and most fantastic concert that will never ever be forgotten!

Elvis' Memphis Mansion—Graceland—as seen in all its splendour.

THE ARCHITECTURAL HISTORY BEHIND
Graceland

If we stretch the point just a little and call his guitar a "harp", Elvis has made it. He's got a mansion, a harp, and a crown! And surely every fan knows that mansion. As *Ideal* magazine has said, "Graceland may be one of the most famous houses in American history". What fan is unaware of that familiar stone house in Memphis, so homelike despite its grandeur? We have all lovingly watched the shrubbery grow as we viewed succeeding photographs. We have a pretty good idea how many swimming pools it has (2), and we know that there is a 75-foot ballroom. There are numerous small houses and outbuildings on the grounds, and many of Elvis' relatives live and work there. It is his *home*, and the fans honour it as such. Elvis has added a screening room, a huge gamesroom, and a network of special paths where he can relax by riding horseback or by scooting around on his go-carts! The grounds cover 14 acres, and in the beginning it all cost him $100,000.

In style, Graceland blends the pseudo-classic, somewhat pretentious southern Antebellum with something of the simple hand-crafted look of a pioneer culture. The latter is provided by the stone. Stone is always in harmony with its environment, and I feel that a stone house can hardly help but have the loved and lived-in look. The house breaks tradition here and there—an almost Spanish touch in the balcony, some Baroque in the statuary, and mid-twentieth-century Arthur Murray in the famous gates—but what would Elvis Presley be without a break with tradition?

I made that last remark with my tongue in cheek, for the fact is that Graceland is very traditional, and to understand its full significance we would have to go back into history, back to the days when "the old south" was in full bloom.

*   *   *

"It was a land of cavaliers . . .", so began *Gone With The Wind*, conjuring up in a phrase an image of the old south as a land where people spent their lives dancing beneath giant chandeliers, riding to the hounds, or sitting on the porch sipping mint juleps. It was a dream world, in which girls as pretty as Scarlet O'Hara, gowned in enormous hooped skirts and wide-brimmed hats, could make one forget that the life of leisure enjoyed by those on top was bought at the price of uncompromising labour and loss of freedom and dignity on the part of the slaves at the bottom. Yet people actually did live that dream. That upper caste did exist, and they held the wealth and power of the south. Partly because of their affluence and partly because they made use of their leisure to enrich their lives with education and the refinements of their culture, they created an ideal for the southern white. In a way they created an ideal for the entire world, even among those nations where slavery was viewed as morally wrong. The apparently glam-orous life of the plantation owners struck chords of envy in those chained to humdrum jobs in industrial cities or bound to dusty toil on the small owner-operated farms of the mid-west. Outsiders saw the romance and missed the fact that the southern life-style was actually filled with superficiality and mannerisms as well as with the dullness of isolated country life. It was also leading to the erosion of soul which comes to any man who keeps another man in chains. It was a medieval feudal system in which the lord owned his serfs and they were chained to the land and subject to his whim. But it was not always a wicked system. Many slave owners educated their slaves and treated them well. In the days before independence the southerners didn't philosophise about slavery or its place in their economic system. They took it for granted, and it wasn't until they found themselves subject to criticism and threat from the north that they began to look for rationalisations to support their way of life.

The Declaration of Independence was signed in 1776, and America was gung-ho for democracy, equality and freedom, and the northerners wasted no time in going to bat against slavery. Now forced to find rationalisations for a system which had done them well, the southern planters looked to Greece. Had not the Greeks managed to run their great civilisation only because they had slaves to do the menial work? Only aristocrats could develop a high culture, and aristocrats must not waste time and energy in menial labour. They began to call themselves "The new Athenians".

There is a direct connection between these things and the architecture which became characteristic of the south. The houses in which we dwell always reflect our society at a given time, for they are, after all, one of the things most intimately connected with our daily lives. They become mirrors of history, and sometimes dig deeper than we know into the meaning of life.

In order to understand southern architecture one must begin in England, for it is in England that the style originated. The first roots are to be found in the Georgian style which was so popular in Britain during the 18th century. Based on classic rules of balance, and proportion, it was preferred by men of fashion and breeding. It became a hallmark of a superior way of life. But let's take a look at what was happening in America about this time. America was not the country it is now, of course. In the 17th century, most of the people were small farmers and numbered about 260,000. By 1760 there were 1,500,000 people in the colonies, and they were not all farmers. There were merchants, shipbuilders, professional men and industrialists among them. The south was still a plantation economy, but everywhere there was a "new aristocracy". There were some artists, some newspapers being published, even a few magazines. Trade with England brought in fabrics,

porcelain, furniture, wallpaper—and housebuilding books! From 1681 on, America was importing not only architectural styles but architects from England. Up until then they had been content with the homespun medieval styles of New England Colonial architecture, and a sprinkling of Dutch styles and the well-known Swedish log cabin design. Now came an influx of British-designed homes of splendid red brick, as Georgian swept over America. But it wasn't many years (1776, you'll remember) before America won her independence from Britain, and the Georgian style passed out of favour. The north revolted against it because it was "royalist" —it bore a king's name. The south were anxious to have a style more distinctly their own, a statement of defiance against the northern abolitionists.

Fortunately, two new colonial styles were fast developing. Southern colonial began in Maryland, Virginia, and the Carolinas, where they built storey-and-a-half homes of brick often with decorative brick masonry, sometimes with large projecting chimneys. Every bit as splendid as Georgian, they tended to more grace and beauty, and they soon spread in the south. They were decidedly more Greek in flavour, and they had a distinct advantage. You could impose the style upon the Georgian house you already owned by simply adding verandahs, porches, or piazzas ringed with pillars or topped with columned porticoes, and these things lent themselves to relaxation and entertaining in the southern climate. Anxious to consolidate their image as "new Athenians", the southerners were ecstatic.

Yet another colonial style was brought in by the French, who settled Louisiana, and it was perhaps the most gracious of all. It was based on the stone architecture of France as it had developed in the New World in Quebec, Canada. (The earliest impressive structure was Champlain's *Habitation* at Port Royal, Nova Scotia, in 1604.) Imported to Louisiana, the style was adapted to the southern climate. Built long and low, as were all of the classic homes, their houses had thick walls of stone and windows shaded by two-storey porches lined with pillars which reached right from the ground, creating a shady space to escape the heat. The style became known as the "Plantation" style, and was popular through the plantation belt in Louisiana and into Mississippi and the surrounding area. Where the early style, the Georgian, had respectability, assurance, and firmness, the southern colonial had added a romantic warmth. Now the French

tecture for the first time, might remark, "How proud. How elegant. Ah, yes! It was a land of cavaliers." And the echoes still ring down the corridors of time. For a long time it was the tragedy of the south that they met defeat in the civil war. They couldn't really admit the defeat because they believed that, as gentlemen, they should have been naturally superior in war, and so they couldn't really believe they had been defeated. They were left with two choices: to forge ahead, join the enemy, change with the times—or to reject change and cling to the past, trying to recapture the glamour of a life-style that was no more, and which had never been, save for the very few. The south chose the latter, and they paid the price for many years. But once you have a myth, you have also an ideal. How easy it is to imagine that a southern child could grow up longing to recapture the glory of that dreamlike and unrealistic past.

No child, despite his individual intelligence or sensitivity, can escape the dominant values of the culture which surrounds him. Elvis Presley was raised in a steaming hot shack in Tupelo, Mississippi, moved into slightly more adequate housing in Memphis, and was jolly lucky to get a high school education. Is it any wonder that he would buy a southern mansion? Some stars, rolling in millions as Elvis has been, might have bought a home of modern design, maybe clinging to a mountain slope on the west coast. Others might have purchased one of the monstrosities of mixed metaphor and hideous taste which appealed to the film greats of the 20s and 30s. Not Elvis. Elvis chose one of the most tasteful homes to be found in America—the southern colonial. And I say that despite the fact that some critics have laughed at his choice, seeing it as a pretention. Well, Graceland *is* a bit pretentious, but all the American buildings of pseudo-Grecian design might be subject to that criticism, including the White House. It's true that Graceland has two modified Corinthian columns supporting a classic cornice and pediment decked in dentils, and that the door is flanked by six pilasters and topped, not with a fanlight, but with a broken pediment and entablature. Do we let this rarified elegance bother us? Not at all! As far as the writer is concerned, Elvis' home, long and low and graceful, balanced with exacting formality, overdressed in the Classic tradition, constructed of good solid stone in the Plantation tradition, is impressive, quiet, homey and almost perfect. After all, it's Graceland!

tempered the original dignity with an almost decadent ease.

So we see that the well-known "southern mansion" is a blend of colonial styles which took root in the American south and became a trademark of the area. To this day, the long, low house, formally balanced with exactly matching windows exactly spaced on either side of a centrally located door, and usually enhanced by pillars, is the most popular style for a new home in the Carolinas, Tennessee, and other southern states. Why? America teems with architects who can produce designs in every idiom from Spanish and Japanese to cubist to space age. Glass and steel and baked enamel and every combination of wood and concrete can be used to bring variety to architecture. Why does the south cling to a long-ago, conformist style? Is it to uphold the tradition that the south is distinctly southern, something "different" in a rapidly changing society? Is it to point out the essential character of hospitality of which the south is proud? What does the southern mansion really symbolise?

Someone who knew nothing of southern architecture or of southern history, seeing the archi-

KAY PARLEY

MY LAS VEGAS

I was conscious of the warm night air as my friend Janice and I made our way to the Hilton Hotel in Las Vegas to see the last show of the Elvis Summer Festival. Two days later, on 4 September, we would be moving on to Los Angeles to complete the last stage of our holiday with the EP Fan Club and although we were looking forward to seeing the sights of LA we were nostalgic at the thought of leaving and hoped our last night at the Hilton would be one to remember.

As we look back some four months later we realise, without doubt, that it was.

We were bubbling over with excitement as we stood "in line" awaiting our turn to go into the Hilton's major showroom, determination to get a front seat increasing as the line moved forward.

At last inside, we asked the waiter if he could find us seats near the cat-walk at the centre of the stage. Unfortunately when we approached that area we could see all the seats were taken and the waiter found us "temporary" seats at the rear of the showroom with the promise that he would squeeze us in at the front after the show started.

We sat there with baited breath, but soon we were escorted to seats at a front table to the right of the cat-walk; our seats being fourth and fifth from the stage facing centre—the table accommodating seven or eight people either side. (Actually, I had been placed near to the front the evening before but the seat had been a great deal further to the right of the stage and I hadn't been able to see a thing.) From these seats we had a clear view.

Eventually the moment we had all been waiting for arrived—Elvis appeared on stage and walked past us on his way to the centre. All eyes followed him and we hoped he would walk over to our side sometime during his performance.

Within a few moments of starting his first number he began to walk slowly towards us. I was so excited, I thought I was going to pass out

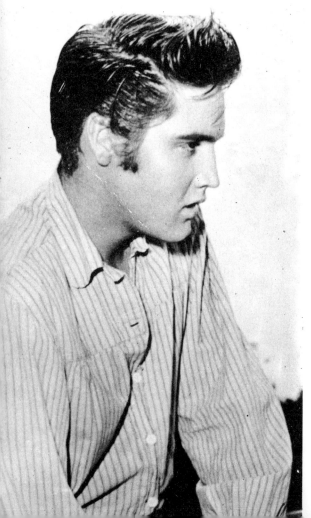

because I had been very upset the first time I had seen him even though I wasn't this close. After pausing to turn around in front of us, he walked back to the centre and my friend whispered, "If you hold your hand out, when he comes over here again, he'll give you a scarf".

It wasn't long before he began singing his way towards us again, but this time he handed out scarves to some of the hands which were going up from all directions. By the time he reached our table the song had finished and he just stood there looking at us. Both of us were speechless but each held out a hand to him. He smiled and said, "Two?" We nodded in agreement and he put his thumb up to let us know we "were on".

He took the scarf he was wearing from around his neck and handed it to me. Then he took another one from Charlie Hodge who had followed him along with a back-up stock, wiped it around his neck, leaned over the edge of the stage and offered it to my friend. Before she could take it someone else from the next table snatched it out of his hand. Elvis, momentarily startled by this unexpected snatch out of the blue, almost lost his balance but straightened up quickly to save himself. In doing so he saw that Janice

Elvis had really gone to a lot of trouble for us. I have never seen Janice so happy—she looked on top of the world.

Satisfied his efforts were successful, Elvis strolled away to get on with the show and my friend, after being prompted by me, sat down abruptly to disappear from the limelight. Unfortunately the "girl of the moment" forgot we were all huddled together and landed in my seat leaving hers spare. A lady gestured her to move down but, misunderstanding the signal, Janice searched the floor and finding nothing (except feet!!) replied, in low tones, that "it" wasn't there! . . . The truth suddenly dawned and order was restored.

From the cheers and applause it was obvious that everyone in the audience had a great time that evening but I feel we had much more—Elvis had made my dream come true and I shall never wash that scarf as long as I live.

SHEILA JONES

didn't have the scarf and after going through the same procedure again, resumed his position at the edge of the stage this time looking around for a simpler way of reaching her.

By now the people sitting on the first three seats at our side of the table had noticed what he was trying to do and we all leaned back out of the way so Janice could move forward.

With the way now easier and the audience stunned by the silence, Janice and Elvis stretched towards each other. When he thought Janice was holding the loose end of the scarf Elvis tossed the end he was holding over her arm.

HOW I MET ELVIS

Jimmy Savile talks to Radio Luxembourg's Duncan Johnson about his early life with Radio Luxembourg, and his meeting with the King in Hollywood. This interview was originally broadcast by Radio Luxembourg during their 40th anniversary programme "This Is How it All began", on Thursday 31st October 1974.

"A record which really sort of made me was Elvis' "It's Now Or Never". By this time I had been on Luxy for about eighteen months, and I was getting very crafty like all Radio Luxembourg disc jockeys. And I thought how can I do something with that Elvis Presley because at that time nobody had ever met him, and this record, after going straight in at Number 1, sold 1,250,000 copies—which is a lot of copies for a British release.

"So that earned him a gold disc to go with about 95 dozen gold discs he already had. But that mattered not at all to me, because here was I, a struggling disc jockey wondering how to take a piece of life and make it come good for me. And that meant that I would have to do strange things. It's no good if you're a disc jockey sitting on your backside yacking words into a microphone, because you've got to get out and do things.

"I took a ticket to Los Angeles, and I arrived in L.A. clutching this gold disc, not the faintest idea where Elvis Presley was—the only thing I knew was that you couldn't ever get to see 'im. I thought, well, we can have a go. I finished up making a phone call to a film studio where I'd heard he was making a film, and a voice said that I could bring the disc 'round there.

"I was twenty minutes late! It was the Paramount film studios actually. I went 'round there in fear and trembling as much as a Yorkshireman can be in fear and trembling; and I was introduced to the Colonel, Tom Parker. He said, 'Are you the guy from England?' 'Yes' I replied. 'You're late!' 'Yes I know, Colonel, because it's 6,000 miles and the traffic was a bit heavy over the last 200 yards.'

"He looked at me, as a character, you see. I stood there with a straight face. He said, 'Stay with me'. I walked 'round the set with him for about half an hour and he kept turning and looking at me. I never uttered a word, me. He said 'Bring the Boy'. The next minute El materialized out of the gloom of this big barn of a studio, and he stood there by the side of me.

"I said, 'Er, I've come to give you this record, and I know that you've got several of them, but I thought that I'd just bring it over, you see. It's a long way, but it's nice to meet you!' What can you do with an opening like that? It's a bit innocent to say the least—

at the time I was as crafty as a fox but I knew when to use an innocent opening. So the Colonel said, 'Bring a picture man,' and lo and behold I finished up with a picture of me and El standing side by side shaking hands. The first ever picture of a British person ever in contact with the guy, shaking hands with 'im. It might mean nothing now, but then it was an unbelievable world-beating thing.

"So I flew back with that picture, which was as precious as gold. Now you might think, that that was enough. It wasn't, because I had a lot of 'em printed and sold 'em. And we got £150.00—which was a lot of money in those days.

"I then gave that £150.00 to the Duke of Edinburgh's Playing Fields Association. So far, so good. But, I phoned Buckingham Palace, and I said that a lot of young people had contributed to this £150.00, and asked, 'Is it possible for me to come 'round and give it to you?' The reply was, 'Certainly, His Highness won't be around because he's away,' and I continued, 'Well it doesn't matter because 'is personal appearance fee is about ten-grand, not one hundred and fifty quid.' You know what I mean, them Royal family, they come a bit expensive!

"You see how I've gone. I've taken a chance, met the Elvis, copped the picture—a lot of people would have stopped there—no, I've come back, I've sold the picture, and now I'm going 'round to Buckingham Palace.

"So I said to my top boss at the time, a gentleman called Mr. S. A. Beecher-Stevens, 'Beech, would you accompany me to Buckingham Palace?,' whereupon his tonsils shot around his head like earrings, and he said, 'Buckingham Palace, what are you talking about?'

"I finished up in morning dress, and the boss in morning dress in Buckingham Palace. When the fella had got the 'undred and fifty pounds, he said 'Right I'll take you out now,' and I said, 'No, I know the way out, it's alright,' and I left the guy's office.

"Now that let me loose, with a very nervous, and petrified boss. And I said, 'Don't go that way, go this way.' 'But Jimmy, this is the way out,' and I said, 'Yes but this is the way in!'

"We went for an hour's walk 'round the corridors of Buckingham Palace, and we finished up at the big double front doors. Now, I claim to be one of the few men, other than the Royal Family to watch the Changing of the Guard from the back!

"All the people, the thousands of people outside the gates, are looking in, and saying 'Which one of the Royal Family is that,' because nobody knew me very much then. My boss, he stood behind the doors daring not to show his face, and said, 'Will you come in? You'll get us shot!'

"When the guards started to walk towards me, I thought that was the time to get the hell out of it. So I retraced my steps, got back into my car in the courtyard, shot off . . . and that's a lesson on HOW TO GET ON WHEN YOU'RE A DISC JOCKEY!"

Pencil sketch by A. M. Bury

ELVIS PERSONAL ALBUM

Vintage 1960

Bottom right: *At the Beverley Wiltshire Hotel while making "G.I. Blues".*

Top right: *At the Hotel Fontainbleu, Miami.*

Below: *At Bad Nauheim, Germany.*

ELVIS PERSONAL ALBUM

Elvis among Fans and Friends

Left: *Fans on the "Graceland" porch, 1960.*

Below: *Outside "Graceland" during the summer of 1958.*

Facing page: *At the Memphis Amusement Park, 1960. Among family, fans and friends you will recognise Anita Wood and Joe Esposito.*

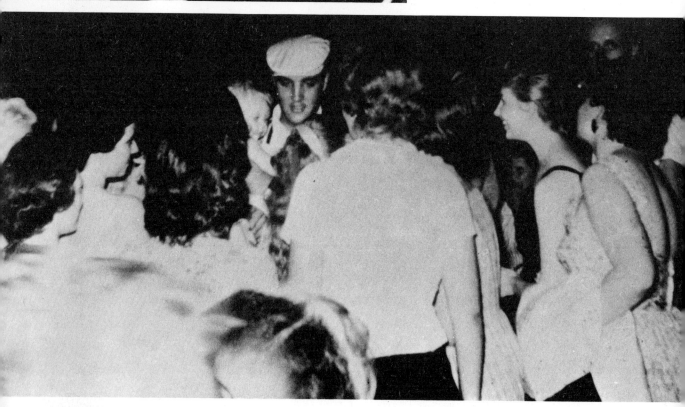

Right: The Memphis Charity Show, with Floyd Cramer, Boots Randolph and Scotty Moore.

Below: Two shots of Elvis with fans at "Graceland".

THE JACKIE GLEASON SHOW

BY TERRY MAILEY JNR.

The Jackie Gleason Shows upon which Elvis appeared in the 1950s were titled 'Stage Shows' and the featured band on them was led by the Dorsey brothers, Jimmy & Tommy. In subsequent years these shows have become known as the 'Dorsey Brothers Shows'.

Elvis first appeared on them on January 28tti 1956 and sang *Blue Suede Shoes,* which he was yet to record for RCA Victor Records, plus his first RCA platter *Heartbreak Hotel,* recorded a mere two weeks before, on January 14th. *Blue Suede Shoes,* Elvis' opening number, was very rhythmic and not as electric as the later recording of it. *Heartbreak Hotel,* Elvis' other number on the show, was very jazzy, similar in treatment to the version he featured in the movie *Elvis–That's The Way It Is.* The Dorsey brothers band backed Elvis on the song, but left Elvis' combo to do the honours on *Blue Suede Shoes.*

A week later on February 4th Elvis re-appeared on the Dorsey show and sang two more songs, these being *Tutti Frutti* and *I Was The One. Tutti Frutti,* which Elvis had recorded on January 30th, less than a week before, was delivered at the same breakneck speed as the single. The song actually featured one of the Dorsey Brothers joining Elvis on the vocals. *I Was The One,* the B-side of *Heartbreak Hotel,* and cut at the same session, was the second song delivered on the show and the Jordanaires were on hand to lend Elvis great vocal support on this their debut song with Elvis.

Februart 11th saw Elvis' third appearance on the show and added another two songs to his growing repertoire: *I Got A Woman* and *Shake Rattle And Roll.* The latter song was performed as per the cut that Elvis laid down on January 30th except that a verse of *Flip, Flop and Fly* was tacked onto the end (rather like Elvis did on his Memphis Live album in 1974). *I Got A Woman,* the first track cut by Elvis for RCA Victor, was performed as per the record, complete with slowed-down ending.

Only one different song was performed by Elvis on his February 18th appearance on the show and this was the 'Sun' classic, *Baby Let's Play House,* which Elvis put over really well. *Tutti Frutti* was performed as per Elvis' February 4th show, the only difference being that the audience seemed wilder this time round, clapping along with the beat of the song.

For the next three weeks Elvis didn't appear on the show, he made his re-appearance on March 17th when he sang *Blue Suede Shoes* and *Heartbreak Hotel. Blue Suede Shoes* was performed as per the RCA version this time around, as too was *Heartbreak Hotel* which just featured Elvis' combo and no Dorsey orchestra.

On Elvis' final appearance on the show on March 24th he sang one last new number, *Money Honey,* along with *Heartbreak Hotel. Money Honey,* which was recorded at the same session as *Heartbreak Hotel,* was performed as per the RCA cut, as was *Heartbreak Hotel* which was a rather shorter version.

All six shows were video recorded and in 1978 the film of the last show surfaced, and for the first time fans outside the USA got the chance to see the raw Elvis on TV in his debut shows and the twenty-two year wait was well worth it. Elvis appeared in an incredibly baggy suit that appeared to have been borrowed from 'Rent-A-Tent', and it soon became obvious why. During each instrumental break he broke loose with his pelvic gyrations and he almost left the screen. It was pure poetry in motion. His grey suit, black shirt and white tie looked menacing and his facial expressions were incredibly sultry and obviously tore the girls of the time up somewhat. Elvis' hair colour was very light, almost blonde and contrasted very well with his dark attire. What a pity he later went dark haired for his first technicolour movie *Loving You,* and stayed that way forever after.

The film of the two songs from the final show was electrifying. Let's hope that fans this side of the Atlantic get a chance now to see the five preceding shows of the Jackie Gleason/Dorsey Brothers programme. It'll be something mind blowing.

An Elvisy Short Story

by Mike Wilkins

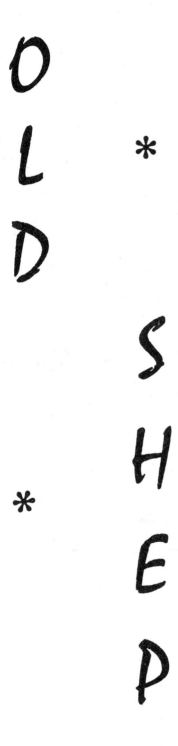

O
L
D
*

*
S
H
E
P

The Tyler family lived in a remote part of the Tennessee countryside. It was difficult to make a living but they managed to live reasonably well despite all the disadvantages. Their success was probably due to the fact that Mrs Tyler was a hard-working woman, not like George her husband who drank far more than he should have done, and did very little work. People often wondered how he managed to find someone as nice as Emma Doyle to marry him.

So twenty years after their marriage, George and Emma lived on the same farm that she had looked after and built up from nothing. George always wanted to live in the town and he made it quite clear that he hated the country and farming. And because he lived so far out of town, he and the eldest son lazed around every day drinking whilst Mrs Tyler went to work in the fields.

The younger son, called various names by his father and brother, was named Jim. And with Jim there was always Shep. Shep was a big shaggy sheepdog. He followed Jim wherever he went; over the hills and meadows. One time Jim fell into the pond and it was Shep who pulled him out, saving him from drowning.

Whilst his father and brother worked little and drank hard, Jim was amazed by their insensitivity to other people and couldn't understand why they should treat both his mother and himself so badly.

One night Jim sat in his room, his mind wandering back over the happy days that were now past, stroking Shep and listening to his few records. These had been given him by his cousin Kathy who lived in the city. He liked playing the slow, sentimental ballads and enjoyed dreaming of the countryside, a peaceful life and a girl. But he always made himself be contented. At least he'd got Shep and his few records. This particular night, his father and brother had gone to town for the night and wouldn't be coming home until the morning. When they did return, he was sure they would be drunk.

The sun, waking from its night's sleep, rose slowly from behind the crimson Tennessee hills.

The earth was still peaceful. Only the sound of a few birds could be heard.

Jim's father and brother were home. More drunk than ever. And he could hear them shouting at his mother. Gently she tried to calm them down. Then Jim's father did something that Jim couldn't stand by and watch – he hit his wife.

"You stinking drunken man," Jim shouted, "you leave Mum alone." George Tyler turned to his son in amazement. Then he lunged forward and beat him with his fists. Jim fell to the floor, hurt and bleeding. After glaring at him for a few seconds longer, his father made straight for Jim's room.

Jim lay on the floor dazed and shocked. Then there was a loud crash. Jim stumbled to his feet and managed to get to the door of his room. His father flung something at him, and then stormed out. Jim sank to his knees and gazed at the pile of broken plastic. Shep came to his side. Not one of his records was in one piece.

George Tyler was sentenced to two years in jail for cruelty to his wife and son. No one ever knew what became of the elder brother. Emma Tyler was treated in hospital for her injuries and because she sold the farm she was able to go to a convalescent home.

Jim went to live with his aunt. It wasn't like home to him, but at least he still had faithful old Shep. They'd always been together through the bad and good times. Every Friday he and Shep would run over the hills, through the forest and across the stream to visit his mother. That's when he was really happy.

Autumn came and the countryside shed its bright green sheen. The fields were brown, amber and gold. The trees had lost most of their leaves and the climate grew colder. Jim was walking home through the wood from school this particular evening . . . without Shep. He was ill and Jim's aunt had called the vet. Jim had been worrying all day about him, but somehow he thought Shep would be all right when he got home. He busied himself reminiscing about the time when Shep's bushy tail had given the show away when he had been scrumping apples from old Jackey's place and was hiding. Jim left the wood and came to the clearing near his aunt's house. His heart banged as he stood for a moment looking at the house. Then he smiled and broke into a run.

"Sheppy, Sheppy old boy, I'm home." Jim reached the porch of the house. Shep's lead was lying on the floor, and he idly picked it up.

With half a smile on his face he entered the house.

"Where's Shep? Is he all right?" he asked.

The vet came over to Jim and smiled sadly. Then his face grew serious.

"I can't do any more for him Jim," he said, and handed him his shotgun. Aghast, Jim let the rifle fall on to the floor.

"I can't do it. I can't do it," Jim cried.

He went up to his room where Old Shep was lying. Jim took him in his arms and held him close for a few seconds and then gently put him down. With tears streaming down his face, and hands trembling he went outside and picked up the gun.

Dusk fell and Jim sat by the old oak tree. The tree which only a short time ago had been a mass of bright green leaves now looked stark and bare. Only a few odd leaves, now browned with age, remained on the damp, rotting branches.

Jim watched a leaf gently fall to and fro, to and fro to the ground. . . .

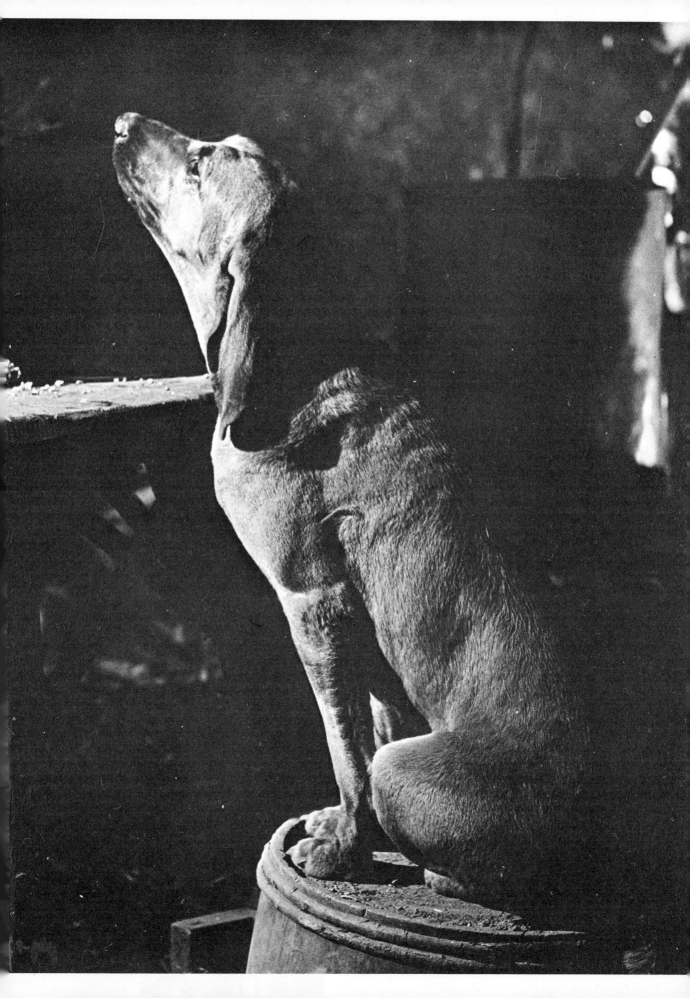

ELVIS - KING of ROCK'n'ROLL?

The tag 'King of Rock'n'Roll' certainly stuck to Elvis throughout his life, yet was he really just worth that tag, or was he more than that? To give Elvis that tag and continually refer to him as such is really an insult to the talent he had. How can you categorise Elvis?

However, Elvis will never be generally thought of as more than that, because how many non Elvis fans have really listened to his music? There are so many people who think only of hits such as *Heartbreak Hotel, Hound Dog, Blue Suede Shoes, Jailhouse Rock.* For some that's all they remember, all they have heard. They have never really listened to the guy.

Elvis was responsible for opening the gates which led to the popular music scene that we know today. I think the main reason he is under-rated by some people is that he showed a surprising lack of inventiveness in the later years of his career. All right he had a marvellous talent and style of presenting his music on stage, yet so many of his hits were only re-covers, why didn't we see more new material?

Maybe his talent stopped him because after setting the standard, his talent for doing songs so much better than the original artists took over, in fact it was the biggest part of his career in a way. We would be at pains to find an album with all new material on, that had never been done before by anyone, if we could find one. I think Elvis could have contributed so much more to the music industry if only he had realised his full talent.

Why oh why, did he never take up the pen himself, because I believe he had that talent in the same way that the Beatles had, they left him behind in the music field and it wasn't until such hits as *Suspicious Minds, In The Ghetto, The Wonder Of You,* that Elvis came to the fore again and people started taking his music seriously once more. Not because these songs are all classics in themselves, but because they were given the Presley magic, and he was the first to record them, so are *his* songs.

Then he slipped back again to the re-covers, and then just to show everyone he still had the old fire, along came *Burning Love,* then we had *Take Good Care Of Her, If-You Talk In Your Sleep, Raised On Rock, Moody Blue,* and finally *Way Down.* Maybe some of them didn't do so well, but it did show that Elvis wanted to record new material, he was looking for a new direction when we lost him to that everlasting stage in the sky.

But in a way there is so much material still to be discovered, not only by us, but by the general public, because how can everyone just call him 'King Of Rock'n'Roll' when there are still so many avenues of music that so many people have not heard him sing. Yet on albums if they had heard them they would know why we do not categorise him and call him 'King Of Rock'n'Roll', but just call him King, for his Kingdom is music.

Alan Armes

"You've got the finest boy in the world, Miz Presley, and it's terrible the way they're makin' him work." It was such a statement made by Colonel Parker in 1955 which won him the greatest showbiz prize of all time—the exclusive management contract for Elvis Presley. Throughout Elvis' career the Colonel was always on hand for the occasional quip to make headlines, and while most considered the man to be something of a Svengali, where Elvis was concerned he was something greater than a super-salesman. This is

THE COLONEL'S STORY

compiled from press interviews by Anne E. Nixon and written by Todd Slaughter (secretary of the Official Elvis Presley Fan Club)

Colonel Parker's flair for straight talking, laced with just the right amount of fairground banter, brought as much attention to his negotiating prowess as to his new product—Elvis Presley. And Elvis was a product he was proud to be associated with, so he often boasted of the situation. "The strength of the contract, any contract, is only as good as the relationship. In all my 28 years in showbiz," the Colonel was reported as saying in 1956, "I've never met anything like this boy. My friends keep asking me, 'Who is Parsley?' We started playing some of the smaller places around the gulf, and at first we were sorta lean, but at the start of '56 business picked up. People were beginning to hear about the kid, and the box office has proved it. And our contract with RCA Victor Records must have been the best deal I've ever made. I told Elvis, 'You stay talented and sexy, and I'll make us both as rich as Rajahs.' Elvis recently said to me, 'You've been so good to me, you put a lump in my throat,' so I replied, 'Thank you son, you've put a lump in my wallet.'"

In 1956 both Elvis and the Colonel had to deal with a lot of tasteless criticism, and although the act was taking off like a whirlwind it was frequently reported that the Colonel paid girls to swoon at his early concert appearances. "I don't have to pay them to swoon. They just naturally go for Elvis all by themselves, without prompting of any kind. He's a great favourite with the girls, but he can't chase them all, there's too many of 'em. I don't know of any case when Elvis has had to chase a girl —no more than any normal American boy, with the exception that instead of having to look for dates there are always lots of fans in the theatre."

Elvis' raw stage presentations were often tagged as obscene—the Colonel disagreed: "Elvis doesn't rock 'n' roll. When the teenagers listen to him, they sit in their seats, and soon begin to jump. And that's what his music should be called—sit and jump—he doesn't bump and grind. He undulates, and his undulations come naturally. The music goes round and round, and Elvis goes round with it.

However, the undulating bit is purely incidental. It doesn't sell songs, but it helps. As for this 'Elvis the Pelvis' stuff, just let me say this—everyone has a pelvis."

"MY BOY DOESN'T NEED DOPE—HE NEEDS SOOTHIN' SYRUP."
So by now you will see the kind of man the Colonel intended himself to be, at least in the public eye. Off duty, he's no hard nut, and his 50 years in show business must have made him the world's most interesting impresario. We've put together, in question and answer form, what must now be the most comprehensive interview with Colonel Parker, compiled from press comments over the years:

1956
How do you attribute your success with Elvis? "Don't let anyone tell you that I made the boy what he is today. The kids are the ones who made Elvis. Without them, he'd still be driving a truck."

Although the girls love Elvis, what about the girls' boyfriends? "Well they have a choice. If they like Elvis, then that's all well and good. If they throw things at him on stage, then we never have to fetch the police—the girls always get there first."

How much tax is Elvis paying these days? "It's not so much a question of how much Elvis makes, it's more a matter of what they allow him to keep."

You are a millionaire manager for Elvis—why do you still maintain your own souvenir concessions? "I'm only filling a need. These people want autographs and pictures, and I'm providing them. I'm not cheating them, am I? I'm giving them what they want, and asking a fair price."

We would like to publish Elvis' life story, is that possible Colonel? "That's mighty nice of you, young man, but tell me one thing, do you want the $2,500 version or the $5,000 story?"

On one occasion the producer of a top-networked US TV programme asked the Colonel if Elvis would guest on his show. The Colonel asked, "Do

other famous fellas appear for nothing?"

"For prestige," was the reply.

The Colonel asked again, "So, do the show's producers and sponsors get paid?"

He was told, "Yes, but guests appear for prestige".

The Colonel asks again, "You mean, everyone gets paid on the show, except my poor boy Elvis?"

The producer argued, "How come all the other people do it for nothing?"

The Colonel concluded, "It's like I've always said, what some people need is a good manager! I'll tell you what, if you want my boy to do two songs then the price is $50,000, but I'll tell you what I'll do. I'll flip you—double or nothing."

The producer declined.

What is your opinion on impersonators, Colonel? "That's a compliment in the entertainment world. When you are mimicked, you know you're a success. Besides, they do us a good service. I don't want to over-expose Elvis—any artiste who is red hot shouldn't be seen too much by the public—so the impersonators keep the ball rollin'."

One day when the Colonel was dining out at 20th Century-Fox's executive restaurant he handed over a gift to Pat Boone. "Give these four Elvis balloons to your daughters—I hear they like my boy."

1957

All the Colonel's contracts are written in large letters to avoid anyone complaining about mis-understanding the 'fine print'. The Colonel says, "All anyone has to do to understand our contracts is to be able to read". In 1957 the Colonel sent the first of many cables to the British Presley Fan Club. It read, "Please thank everyone for being so loyal to Elvis. We sincerely appreciate everything you and your associates are doing. Please thank all the members for all of us."

Colonel, another year has passed, and you must be another million dollars richer—why can't you employ someone to sell your programmes? "I like doing it, and anyway some people like to say that they bought their programme off the Colonel. You know, I've never seen the end of any of Elvis' pictures? Ten minutes before they finish I always have to rush out to sell photos of Elvis to the folks coming out. When I met Elvis he had a million dollars worth of talent—now he has a million dollars."

1958

When Colonel Parker saw Elvis off into the American army, he decided to de-rank himself for a week, calling himself Private Parker. "But, you'll bet it'll be my patriotic duty to keep my boy Elvis up in the supertax bracket while he's in the army. Not that he'll be joining the special services, and entertaining the other troops—a sure way to debase your merchandise is to give it away."

"Elvis was good enough for me before he was in the army, and he's sure good enough for me now—I'm not even taking on another client. Too many people jump off the wagon when it stops, and try to get back on when it rolls again. Me, I'll just keep greasing the wheels. I'm doing everything I can to keep Elvis in front of the folks while he's serving his country. I've been to see him a couple of times. He looks really healthy and tanned. He's doin' fine—'course, he did pretty well when he was pale too."

1959

"My boy has perfect manners, and never steps out of line. After all this time, he's never called me anything but Colonel."

1960

The latter part of Elvis Presley's army life was spent in Germany, but 1960 saw his return to civilian life.

As he arrived at Fort Dix in a snowstorm the Colonel was asked why less than 50 fans were waiting in attendance. "Forty-five in weather like this is like 250 or more in good weather." Still, Nancy Sinatra was there to greet him. "Never mind me, it's Elvis' fans who ought to be praised for staying loyal. He still holds the record for attendance or personal appearance tours of any singer. We feel that with Elvis' stint in Germany, this will improve his status on the international movie and record market. Elvis has come back with high hopes, and we wish to thank the public for their loyalty and kindness." However, the Press were not so kind. This year the Women's Press Club in Hollywood awarded Elvis and the Colonel their Club Raspberry for 'non-co-operation'. The Colonel joked, "Great, when do we get the plaque?"

1961

Privately, like Elvis, the Colonel often supported charities, and on the occasions that he was 'found out' he preferred to brush off the attention. In Hawaii for the Pearl Harbour fund the Colonel gave $14,000 of his own money and when challenged all he would say was, "I was happy to do it, along with Elvis".

Bob Hope often talked about the Colonel. "I don't think there's another man like Colonel Parker in the World." At a recent MGM party the Colonel stood by the door handing out Elvis photos saying, "My boy is in Hawaii making *Blue Hawaii*—a Hal Wallis Production—A Paramount Picture". I ask you, who else would do it at a reception where MGM were picking up the tab?

I understand you've been offered a part for Elvis Presley in a movie which could get Elvis his first Oscar. Why did you decline? "I didn't, I simply said, you give us our price of $350,000 for the picture. If Elvis gets the Oscar, then we'll refund you $50,000. Either that, or we'd roll the dice—double or nothing."

A British promoter has suggested you could play Elvis at Wembley Stadium within a 'goldfish bowl' to magnify him for the audience. "I see one problem with that. If they are going to get an Elvis nine times bigger, then the promoter has got to pay nine times the price. I've also been asked if we are interested in playing Las Vegas hotels again. Not really. Why, to pay us, they'd have to sell the hotel."

"Elvis and me, we go for days sometimes without talking to each other. We have an understanding that is hard for some folks to comprehend. Our contract, made out at the start, is not a binding affair, made out for life. If it had to have those kind

of legal clauses, it wouldn't mean much in the first place. We just go along, working, doing the best we can. Elvis selects all of his own songs for his records, and since they sell like hot cakes, he has good judgement. I don't even attempt to advise him. Elvis has to feel his songs. He has to feel them to sing them the way he does. I never interfere in Elvis' personal life. What goes on with him away from business, I don't know. When people ask if we have a press agent to report on Elvis' personal life, I say we don't have one. Take Elvis' records, we could keep putting them out every week. We limit them to four a year. We keep him off TV by asking $150,000 an appearance, and of course, if someone wants to pay it, then we can't deprive them."

1962

When the Colonel found out that there was no roof on a stadium where he thought he might play Elvis, he asked for an extra clause in the contract. "In the event of rain—we will have the concession to sell umbrellas." It was these 'extra clauses' which often got the Colonel out of embarrassing situations.

1963

"My boy had one hobby last year. He has the same one this year, and it'll be the same next year—pretty girls. I've met Ann-Margret, and she's real pretty, but there'll be others to follow." The Colonel would never break a confidence about a Presley romance.

What do you think, Colonel, about Elvis' role in Kissin' Cousins? "I liked the idea of a dual part, but I guess the film company didn't fall in line with my suggestion that he should be paid the normal fee for each of the two parts."

"I've never attended a recording session. When he's in the studio it's always late at night, so I'm in bed asleep. I figure there's nothing I can do to contribute to his recording. I'm much better getting my sleep, so that the next day I'm alert and ready to do the deal that will bring in some more money for my boy."

1964

In 1964 Elvis' passion for collecting police badges was becoming a regular hobby. On one occasion he rang the Colonel to boast that he'd won another badge, and had been made an honorary sheriff. The Colonel replied, "Good, but don't you come back here giving me tickets for anything". In the same year a producer rang the Colonel begging that he read a new film script. "If you want me to read a script, that'll be $10,000 extra."

1965

This was the year it was suggested in *Elvis Monthly* that Elvis might be Welsh. The Colonel was quick to comment. "If it makes my boy Elvis get more money—I'll make him Welsh, quick like."

Tell me, Colonel, why did you turn down the British Royal Variety Performance? "Let's find out first whether the Queen really wants to meet Elvis. If she doesn't, then we've no right to go. If Elvis goes to Britain, it would have to be for a 100% charity show. Someone would have to give the theatre free of charge—even the popcorn seller would have to turn over his profits."

1966

"Would you like to hear a song I wrote. I call it 'The Producer's Lament'. It goes . . . Elvis loves us, yes we know. He promised us a show. The Colonel stopped it—there was no dough."

"A guy started talking about Brian Epstein, and I said, I wished I was as smart as he is. He's got four guys, and I've only got one. But I wouldn't swop that one for anything."

"Elvis hasn't done a personal appearance in five years. His films can be seen by fans the world over. People say Elvis' films aren't doing so well. We've made 22 pictures, and 19 have been great big box office successes—two have still to complete their run, and one hasn't been released yet. If his pictures aren't doing so successfully how come all the people who made them want him back for more? I never look at scripts—Elvis does that. If Elvis hasn't found the right script yet, he's earned a lot of money trying over the past 10 years. How else could I pay for our Christmas trade ads in papers like the *NME* if I didn't get the money?"

"If Elvis decides to get married, he'll have to tell me first, so I can up the price on our pictures—after all, there'd be an extra mouth to feed."

AND SO ON . . .

In 1967 Elvis finally married, and perhaps the Colonel decided that he'd said enough, but he still continued to play fast and loose with the entertainment business. One of the nicest stories concerns the Colonel being able to collect $50,000 from a TV network for a non-appearance. He told the producer, "I'm considering an offer from another network, but for $50,000 you can buy his exclusive TV services for the next 90 days—that way you can't use him, but you can make sure he won't work for the other networks". The producer? He paid up.

Television brought Elvis back to the people, and the completion of the International Hotel in Las Vegas put Elvis back before live audiences, which paved the way to nationwide tours. "Many people in many places don't get a chance to see Elvis'

dynamic act. They can't fly to Las Vegas, so we're doing the next best thing, and flying Elvis on film to them. Dennis Sanders is making *Elvis, That's The Way It is* for MGM, but I told him, now don't you go winning no Oscar with this picture, because we don't have no tuxedos to wear to the celebration."

US comedian Pat Henry often tells the story of his meeting with the Colonel. "He gave me a small picture calendar of Elvis and said, 'We usually charge for these, but I like you, so I'm giving it to you free of charge—don't tell Elvis!'"

TODD SLAUGHTER'S OBSERVATIONS

On the numerous occasions I've met with Colonel Parker we've rarely talked about Elvis. The Colonel obviously reads a lot of newspapers because he's always up to date with the state of the British economy, and we'd spend hours discussing the problems of the world. I was in Los Angeles once and the Colonel decided he wanted a hamburger. There was one problem—there was a bread strike. Such a problem didn't bother the Colonel— we drove for about an hour to find a restaurant which baked its own bread, and so the Colonel got his hamburger.

I remember the Colonel holding up his CBS TV discussions until the company had agreed to include 300 polystyrene hats for Elvis' British fans in the contract. And when they questioned the possibility of broadcasting the TV programme's sound simultaneously on stereo radio, the Colonel refused by simply saying, "The network doesn't have enough money!"

1977

Colonel Parker was on tour when Elvis died in Memphis on 16 August. Joe Esposito called Parker from Graceland, and the Colonel flew to Memphis to take charge of the funeral plans. But no one saw the Colonel. There were no interviews, no press comments, nothing. The Colonel even refused to drive in the lead mourners' cars, and when asked why he didn't wear a suit and tie to the funeral, the man replied, "I couldn't wear a suit, why, if I did Elvis wouldn't have spotted me in the crowd".

"If I shed a tear for Elvis when he died, no one saw it. Why, if they had, they would have had their hands in our pockets quicker than that. Before it was Elvis and the Colonel. Now it's Elvis, Vernon Presley and the Colonel. Thank you all for your everlasting loyalty."

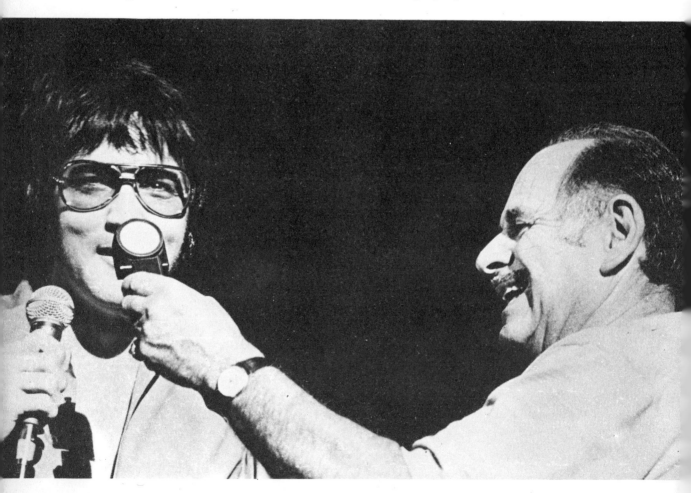

ELVIS' SUN CAREER

Regarded as the most important stage in his entire career, the fact remains that Elvis was only with Sun for fourteen months, signing on in July 1954, and moving to RCA-Victor in November the following year.

Perhaps the most significant aspect of his short association with Sam C. Phillips' Sun label was that when he walked in off the street he was about as enterprising as a rank amateur could be, straight out of the crackerbarrel, with no previous experience, content to just learn the latest radio and Soda shop juke box hits, and try them out at home on his beat-up guitar. "A snot-nosed wild kid" was how the late Bill Black referred to Presley after their initial meeting.

Officially there were only five Presley singles issued on Sun Records to be re-cycled when RCA-Victor bought out Phillips' interests, and they were "That's All Right", "Blue Moon Of Kentucky", "I Don't Care If The Sun Don't Shine", "Good Rockin' Tonight", "Milk Cow Blues Boogie", "You're A Heartbreaker", "I'm Left, You're Right, She's Gone", "Baby Let's Play House", "Mystery Train" and "I Forgot To Remember To Forget".

Phillips did not begin to file regular session details until 1958, preferring to jot things down in his personal notebook. As a result vital information has been lost. The story goes that when Presley joined RCA, the company were short on current tracks for his debut album, and so decided to examine the tapes they had purchased from Phillips and put out "I Love You Because", "Blue Moon", "I'll Never Let You Go", "Just Because" and "Trying To Get To You". Their logic being that this was the sound that had prompted them to buy out Sam C. Phillips in the first place, so why not get a quick return on their original outlay?

Now, here's where the saga gets somewhat blurred. Some sources insist that RCA-Victor acquired everything except the Million Dollar Quartet tapes (more about that later), while others maintain that Phillips still has in his possession innumerable out-takes, incomplete masters and rough demos. The recent appearance of an exquisitely produced Dutch bootleg album, adds to the confusion. This has one entire side devoted to the original commercial takes of "Good Rockin' Tonight", "Mystery Train" and "I Forgot To Remember To Forget", plus two false starts and the completed version of "I Don't Care If The Sun Don't Shine"—an alternate countrified workout of "Blue Moon Of Kentucky", the previously bootlegged sloweddown version of "I'm Left, You're Right, She's Gone", known as "My Baby's Gone", a hitherto unknown split tempo arrangement of "I'll Never Let You Go", interspersed with brief snatches of chit-chat in the Sun Studio at 706 Union Street. In the summer of 1953 Elvis was driving a Ford pickup truck for the Crown Electric Company of Memphis for around 42 dollars a week. On one Saturday he stopped by the Memphis Recording Service. Running the Memphis Recording Service office was Marion Keisker who charged four dollars to cut a double-sided 10-inch acetate. Business was always brisk, especially at weekends, so Presley got in line behind the local starstruck hill jacks to wait his turn. Then after paying his four bucks, he proceeded to perform The Inkspots' "My Happiness" and "That's When Your Heartaches Begin" to his own acoustic guitar accompaniment. On hearing Presley's voice Keisker managed to get the last part of "My Happiness" and the whole of "That's When Your Heartaches Begin" onto a discarded length of recording tape.

Clutching his finished acetate Presley said "goodbye"—he was always polite—and turned off in his truck. Phillips was away at the time, but when he returned Keisker played him the rough tape. The boss was impressed, but had some reservations. He figured this singer needed a lot of grooming but he did make a note of Presley's address, 462 Alabama Street.

On Friday, 4 January 1954, Presley again dropped by Memphis Recording Service with another four dollars and his guitar. This time Keisker was out but Phillips was in. Presley recorded "Casual Love" and "I'll Never Stand In Your Way" and was in and out within half an hour.

Almost eight months to the day after Presley's initial visit to Memphis Recording Service, Phillips received the dub of a song called "Without You" cut in Nashville by an unknown negro singer. He liked it, and tried in vain to contact the singer. He called up Presley as a last resort. Studio time was arranged but it proved disastrous. Presley failed to get to grips with either "Without You" or another number called

"Rag Mop".

During a break, Phillips enquired as to what else Presley could do,· and Presley didn't need asking twice. The 18-year-old singer ran the gauntlet of gospel, country and religious songs. Phillips' next move was to call up a 21-year-old guitar picker named Scotty Moore and arrange for him to meet Presley. Eventually Elvis and Scotty met up at the guitarist's house one weekend and messed about on songs by Eddy Arnold and Hank Snow plus a few ballads made popular by Billy Eckstein.

After a couple of hours a bass player called Bill Black, who just lived three doors down, dropped by for a few minutes. But he did not like what he saw of Presley, who was decked out in bright pink shirt 'n' slacks, offset with white bucks and a whole jar of grease on his hair.

On 5 or 6 July, Black found himself in Sun Studio with Presley and Moore for what was supposed to be an audition, but what in fact turned into several months of hard sweat, to develop and perfect a distinctive and commercial style for the singer. Allegedly, the first thing actually taped was "I Love You Because"—a special version of two takes appearing on Presley's debut RCA-Victor album and also coupled with "Trying To Get To You" as a single. The original unedited version (narration and all) surfaced twenty years later on "Elvis—A Legendary Performer" and the "Sun Collection". Other songs laid down included "I'll Never Let You Go" and something called "Satisfied". During a refreshment break Elvis suddenly grabbed hold of his guitar and started fooling around on the old 40s Arthur Crudup tune "That's All Right". Bill Black picked up the rhythmic bass beat and Scotty Moore joined in with appropriate guitar licks.

Nobody was quite sure what they were doing but at Phillips' instigation they quickly did it again—this time with the tapes rolling. It was wildly exciting, but upon hearing the playback the concensus of opinion in the studio was that once the public heard it they'd be run out of town.

Next move was for Phillips to take a selection of dubs over to Station WHBQ disc jockey Dewey Phillips. Dewey by-passed the slower version of "Blue Moon of Kentucky" and chose to preview "That's All Right" over the air. And within minutes the switchboard was jammed.

Dewey was to play "That's All Right" quite a number of times that evening. By 19 July the record was in the local stores, and the end of the month saw it ensconced at the number three slot on the Memphis C & W chart.

As a result Elvis, Scotty and Bill were booked for Nashville's "Grand Ole Opry" and Shreveport's "Louisiana Hayride"—things were on the up and up.

As far as we know, the next recording sessions were arranged sometime in September and produced "Good Rockin' Tonight" and "I Don't Care If The Sun Don't Shine". Now it's quite possible that more sessions were undertaken but were never written down. However, the next session to produce finished material was in December, and the tracks were "Milk Cow Blues Boogie", "You're A Heartbreaker"—with DJ Fontana added on drums—"Baby, Let's Play House" and "I'm Left, You're Right, She's Gone". By July of 1955 DJ Fontana had become a permanent fixture in Presley's entourage, and "Baby, Let's Play House" was on the national bestsellers.

This was the month when the music business moguls began to take notice of the heated controversy Presley was generating through his public appearance, and as far as we know, this was when Presley and his musicians cut their final session for Sun, "Mystery Train" and "I Forgot To Remember To Forget" being issued in August.

Ahmet Ertegun was first to step forward with

a firm offer of 25,000 dollars to woo the hillbilly cat to Atlantic, but in the end it was RCA-Victor's bid of 35,000 dollars plus a five-grand bonus for Presley which was accepted. Though Presley's Sun contract still had one year to run, the agreement made with RCA-Victor stipulated that Sun was to retain the rights to fulfil all orders up until 1 January 1956, after which date the new company would have exclusive rights to everything Phillips had recorded or would record with Presley.

This initial contract was for three years with options.

Now seeing that RCA-Victor did in fact issue a selection of Sun tracks originally rejected by Sam Phillips, it's quite feasible that RCA-Victor must own the cache of unreleased material which allegedly includes "I'll Never Let You Go", the souped-up version of "Oakie Boogie", "Give Me More More More (of your kisses)", "Crying Heart Blues", "Tiger Man" and "Uncle Penn"— which was apparently issued for a couple of days by accident! The story goes that it was put out on a local label as a tryout but flopped with "Night Train To Memphis", "Blue Guitar", "Gone", "Always Late With Your Kisses", "Tennessee Partner", "Rockin' Little Sally", "Sunshine", the oft-bootlegged "My Baby's Gone", "Without Love", "That's The Stuff You Gotta Watch" and "Tennessee Saturday Night". When he departed from Sun, Presley didn't sever all connections, often returning to the Union Street Studio to hang out with his old friends. On one occasion he dropped by a Jerry Lee Lewis session and can be heard adding vocal harmony to the Otis Blackwell composition "Am I To Be The One" ("A Taste Of Country"—Sun 6467015).

Then around Christmas 1956, Elvis and Jerry Lee both played piano, and Johnny Cash and Carl Perkins supplied the guitars, as all four performed a whole selection of gospel and R & B material. Referred to as "The Million Dollar Quartet" it has been verified that these tracks are still in Sam C. Phillips' vault.

In all probability, all the unreleased Presley Sun material supposedly gathering dust in RCA-Victor's vaults isn't up to the standard of his commercial releases, and that's why they've remained unheard.

Nevertheless, someone saw fit to dig out the tape of "I Love You Because", and we've the Elvis Sun Collection, so why can't we get the Million Dollar tapes and the rest of the unreleased Sun and RCA material on to album release?

DEREK LYNN

By Michael Pesce

ELVIS PERSONAL ALBUM

Family and Friends

Top left: *Elvis's father in the grounds of "Graceland".*

Bottom left: *Elvis with Uncle, Johnny Smith and Mrs. Smith at the Rainbow Roller Rink.*

Below: *Cousin, Bobby Smith.*

Right: *With Harris Strickland Jun. at Miami.*

Below: *Elvis's cousin, Patsy Presley.*

Bottom: *Uncle Travis with a gathering at "Grace-land".*

The Year - 1961

Left: *Sunday afternoon on the "Graceland" porch.*

Below: *Leaving for location of "Kid Galahad".*

"Play it James!"

ONE OF THE GREAT SOUNDS BEHIND ELVIS

by
TONY
NEALE

There are many fine guitarists to be found on the music scene these days, people like John McLaughlin, Eric Clapton, Jamie Robbie Robertson, Jeff Beck and Jimmy Page, plus their numerous lesser imitators jostling around, waiting for their chance at super-stardom; but while most people are familiar with the above names, there are many more excellent musicians who, while they aren't feted quite so much by Joe public, nonetheless command considerable respect from their fellow musicians: James Burton is such an artist.

James Burton is not a speed-merchant, nor does he play guitar with his teeth or set fire to it and chuck it through his amplifier, but then he doesn't need to, his talent speaks for itself without the need for outlandish theatrics to underline it. Back in the early days, Scotty Moore served as Elvis' right-hand man, belting out those hair-raising chords on classics like "Lawdy Miss Clawdy" and "Baby Let's Play House", and a guitarist more suited to the dynamic Presley style it would be hard to imagine; I personally dig many different guitar-pickers, including Steve Cropper, mainstay of many a great soul sound from the Memphis-based "Stax" label, Hank Marvin, Duane Eddy, Clapton, Hendrix, (who's slow Blues number: "Red House" would be an ideal song for Elvis himself), and lately the amazing pyrotechnics of Roy Buchanan. But right from the first time I heard that tough, raunchy "Untouchable" sound, Scotty has remained my all time fave-rave axe-man. However, running him a very close second on my list is the subject of this article; when you listen to James Burton he seems to be the only logical successor to Scotty Moore. It's no use saddling Elvis with any of the contemporary pickers because too many of them tend to favour lengthy, improvisational workouts which, while they might be "really far out, man", technically speaking, all too often come across as so much self-indulgent musical wallpaper; a player such as this would swamp Elvis, who has always favoured short, sharp guitar solos, and in this respect Burton is Scotty's equal; I mean he even sounds like Scotty, and what more could anyone ask? It seems amazing to me that it took Elvis and James so long to get around to working together, so compatible are they musically; but then James is much in demand as a session-guitarist and I guess it took

someone of Elvis' stature to lure him away from that lucrative sideline and onto a stage.

James hails from Shreveport, Louisiana, and started out on the famous "Louisiana Hayride" which of course Elvis himself played regularly during the early "Sun" days; says Burton of that time: "I remember seeing some of his early shows when he was just beginning. To me he was fantastic, I'd never seen anything like that in my life. . . . I'll never forget those early shows—it was the real thing!". So James was certainly aware of the young Elvis, but still they never crossed paths at that time.

James must have started out very young on the "Hayride" because he was still only fifteen around 1956–57 when he played on his first big record, supplying the raunchy lead on the Dale Hawkins biggie: "Suzie Q.". Actually, there's recently been some controversy as to whether Burton does play on this recording, but I must say it sure enough sounds like him to me; who else could get that close to his hard, biting sound—'cept maybe Scotty himself, and he was busy turning out some smouldering licks for Elvis at the time!

After the Hawkins record, James then teamed up with a rising young Elvis look-alike teen-idol, Ricky Nelson, and, along with drummer Richie Frost and Bassist James Kirkland turned out some of the finest pop-rock of the late fifties/early sixties. I'm sure most people are familiar with the big Nelson hits such as "It's Late", "Hello Mary Lou" and 'Fools Rush In" etc. . . ., all featuring some of the greatest guitar solos to come out of the Rock'n'Roll era, but the group also laid-down some excellent lesser-known items, many of which can be found on the recently issued Nelson double album in the United Artists "Legendary Masters" series, featuring all the big smashes along with more obscure gems from the vaults. Take a listen to Burton's atmosphere lead on Nelson's version of "My Babe", or the blistering break-neck backing on "Milkcow Blues" and "I Got A Woman". And Burton and Co. come the nearest I've heard to re-creating that classic "Sun" sound on the Johnny Cash-penned number: "Restless Kid"; the sound on this cut is really knockout.

James stayed with Nelson right up until the mid-sixties when Rick kind of lost direction, musically

Sandy Chapman
1971

speaking, for a while and they drifted apart, James concentrating more on session work and Rick eventually returning to his first love, Country music—and forming the Stone Canyon band.

James is perhaps noted more for his Rock style than any other but he can turn his hand to just about anything the situation demands, and he's played with hundreds of different artists, from the late Gram Parsons to Nancy Sinatra, and Sammy Davis to Tom Jones. He can be heard on the second Buffalo Springfield L.P.: "Buffalo Springfield Again", playing dobro on a track called: "A Child's Claim To Fame", and more recently, adding some chilling guitar to a number on the excellent Joni Mitchell album: "For The Roses" called "Cold Blue Steel And Sweet Fire". A year or so back he even got around to finally cutting a solo album for A & M (number SP-4293), which includes instrumental versions of "Mystery Train" (sounding uncannily like Scotty Moore), "Suzie Q", "Fools Rush In", "Johnny B. Goode", "Hound Dog" and "Polk Salad Annie", the latter owing a lot to the live Elvis version. To anyone who digs the sound featured on the recent Presley live sets, especially the up-tempo stuff, this solo L.P. is a must for the collection. Anyhow, they say that as one door closes another opens, and this is true for Burton, who has left the side of one musical legend to join the biggest of them all, and it's hard to imagine Elvis without James by his side now, in much the same way as it was with Scotty and Bill and D. J. Fontana back in the early days.

Since joining Elvis in his first Vegas season four years ago, James has laid down numerous great solos starting with a vengeance on the "Vegas To Memphis" double set, the live half of which features a supreme back-up band with James supplying much of the fire with that biting axe; take a listen to my personal favourite of all the Elvis live cuts so far, the "Mystery Train"/"Tiger Man" medley. The backing is nothing short of sensational, with some especially hard-driving

drum work and, of course, Burton cutting through everything like a knife through butter; the solo on "Mystery Train" is so like Scotty it sends shivers up the spine. Absolute dynamite.

But of course it's not merely on Rock material that James excels, witness the beautifully-mellow solo on "The Wonder Of You" or the poignant, introspective picking on "Funny How Time Slips Away", creating a real empathy between guitar and vocal: great stuff! Then there's the bluesy side of Burton found on the excellent: "Merry Christmas Baby" and "Steamroller Blues", the fine country picking on Dylan's: "Don't Think Twice It's Alright", the tastefully-understated solos on "Spanish Eyes" and "Good Time Charlie's Got The Blues", the short, sharp atmosphere licks on "Find Out What's Happening" and "Just A Little Bit", and not forgetting that aggressively exuberant workout on "Faded Love". In an interview a few years ago, James revealed that Elvis sometimes refers to him jokingly as "Chuck Berry" and it's no wonder when you hear the sounds he produces on the fantastic "Promised Land" single, a perfect showcase for that magnificent Burton magic.

I've always regretted the fact that Scotty Moore seems content to limit his time to a little session-work now and then, giving us little chance to hear once again that unique unforgettable sound; however, if someone has to fill Scotty's shoes I can't think of anyone better than James Burton for the role. When asked, a few years back, what it was like working with Elvis, James replied: "He's a fantastic person. All the time I worked with him he was just great. I'm really looking forward to working with him again". Well he obviously feels the same way now because he's still up there on the boards with Elvis, and in the studio, knocking out that old magic, and I for one hope he remains a permanent fixture on the Elvis scene. In a nutshell, I can do no better than to echo Elvis' own words— "Play it, James"!

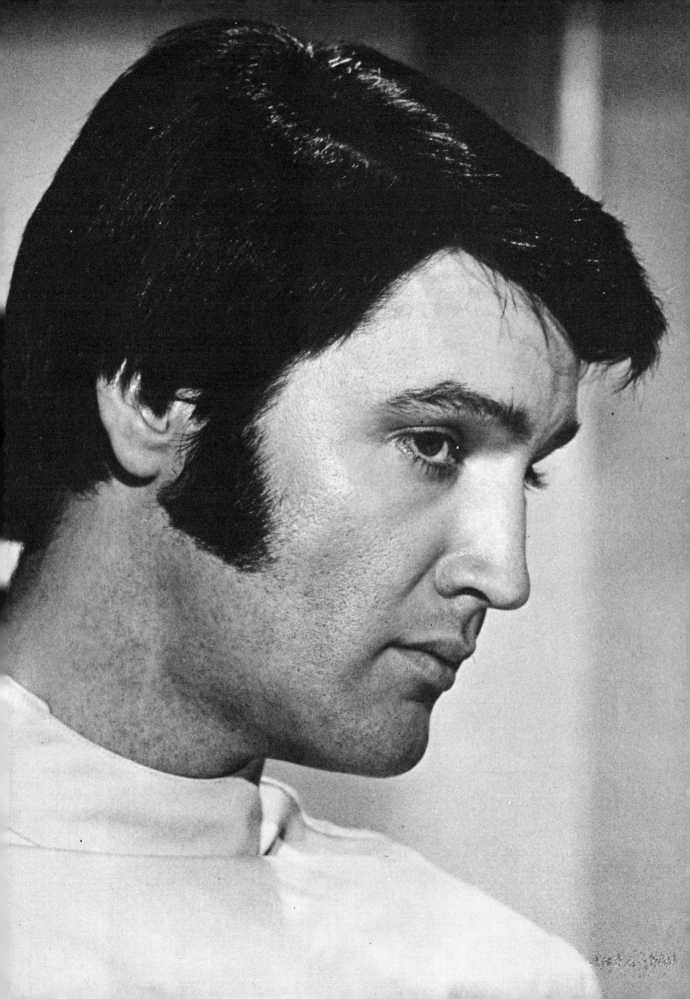

ELVIS ISLAND DISCS

by MARTHA DUNCAN

Have you ever sat down and tried to figure out which eight El discs you'd take to that desert island? Don't bother unless you have hours and hours to spare because it is almost as impossible as trying to empty the Atlantic with a teaspoon.

Number one was easy. "King of the Whole Wide World" because that was the first thing I consciously heard Elvis sing. I *must* have heard his voice before this song if only because we had a radio in the house and I gather that for a while it was pretty well impossible to turn on a radio without hearing him, but all the same I can honestly say that until the day the "King" sent shivers down my spine I was totally unaware of Elvis Presley!

My second choice wasn't too difficult either. I do my exercises to this one and I figure that a desert island would give me plenty of free time to get rid of unwanted fat. Trying to figure out which number I swing from head to toe and back again with? "Can't Help Falling in Love"! Another reason is that this is my husband's favourite Elvis record and that counts.

I would like one from each movie but that would overstep my allowance all by itself! Take

"Roustabout". All good numbers. "Little Egypt"? Good for a laugh any day. The rip roaring "Carny Town"? The title song? No, I'm going to take a song that to me seems to be a little part of Elvis. The song that I can't listen to without catching a glimpse of the scenes behind

the scenes of the Elvis we see on the screen. "Hard Knocks." Oddly enough I can't even remember the scene in which he sang it!

Now one that I can't leave behind. "It Hurts Me."

Half-way there.

I feel that in this choice there should be at least one of the early frantics: "Hound Dog", or "Blue Suede Shoes" or "All Shook Up", but much as I love them they are not the ones that I play most often. These are easy to spot because they are no longer shiny black but a dull worn grey! Like "Puppet on a String" for example . . . I'll take it as my number five providing they give me a new copy!

Then a favourite movie full of favourite songs. "G.I. Blues." But of them all I find myself placing the needle carefully on the last track on side 2. That quiet, unpretentious, almost sad little number "Doing The Best I Can".

Only two more to choose, and how am I going to exist without those bits of records that I love so much? Could I stand being on an island and not have the surf background to "Blue Hawaii"? Could I live without hearing the drums of "Baby I Don't Care"? Or that clattering guitar work behind "Working on the Building"? Or the "whoo" at the end of "Such a Night"?

I sat for ages playing through discs that I was sure I must have and then one jumped out suddenly at me and I realized that I had been so busy replaying the old tried and true that I had forgotten the "newer" one, "Memphis, Tennessee". I don't know how this or for that matter any other record effects other people but when Elvis sings "Mmmmphis" I simply dissolve!

And lastly? Oddly enough I didn't have any trouble choosing this one. In the first place I have never heard Elvis sing it. But not long ago I bought that great Scotty Moore L.P. "The Guitar That Changed the World" and there was "Loving You" and as soon as I heard it I knew that it would take its place in my favourites. If this sounds like a plug for Scotty Moore I am sure Elvis would be the last to object!

You always get one luxury to take with you too, so I'll choose that delightful bar-room scene from "Tickle Me".

O.K.! There's my choice. . . . What's your's?

Wearing that loved on look

BY TERRY MAILEY JNR.

Throughout two decades Elvis was noted for his gaudy attire, from street wear to stage wear. From the tips of his toes to the tip of his head (e.g. outlandish socks and slick hats), whatever he wore was a topic of conversation. In this article I plan to look back over some of the memorable clothes that have been associated with Elvis over the years.

On stage in the very early days Elvis was noted for wearing extremely baggy trousers and jackets that were at least one size too big for him. The reason for this was quite simple, Elvis needed the extra room to move around in when he was performing his wild stage act. The trousers were mostly black whilst the jackets were usually tweed and in a wide variety of colours: blue and white striped with a black velvet collar, grey with silver specks in it, green and sometimes even pink. When the jackets were sombre Elvis usually wore an eye-catching shirt to highlight them. The black shirt with the white polka-dots is a famous one, as too is the one with the checks in it. When Elvis didn't wear a jacket he usually wore a shirt that stood out on its own and surely his most famous one was the velvet shirt that he wore at his Tupelo show in 1956, the same one that he wears on the cover of the British album *Elvis, Rock And Roll Vol. Two* (HMV).

Movies produced some great clothes and none better than the technicolour movie, *Loving You.* Whoever can forget the 'Teddy Bear' outfit, or the brown suede studs that Elvis wore whilst singing *Mean Woman Blues.* Even in black and white his clothes looked striking. The *Baby I Don't Care* jumper, the all black attire of *Dixieland Rock,* complete with neck choker.

Street wear consisted of leather jacket when he was out riding his motorcycle in and around Memphis, and his favourite loud clothes from his favourite store. The most famous attire of the 1950s however must surely be the famed gold lamé suit, a creation inspired by Liberace whom Elvis saw in 1956 when he appeared at the New Frontier in Las Vegas. The suit which is in magnificent colour on the *Touch Of Gold* E.P.s and the album, *Elvis' Gold Records Vol. Two* is absolutely stunning.

For two years Elvis was in the army, however in army uniform he looked more than just an average G.I. He had that certain something that made anything he wore look like a million dollars, even army khaki.

Following Elvis' army service a more mature Elvis re-appeared on the music scene, one that wore Italian tailored suits and snazzy Sinatra style hats. Even in these though he looked slicker than ever and when upon his return to Las Vegas he got into jumpsuits he outdazzled even the brightest shining star. Each subsequent stay in Vegas brought forth a different suit, as did the many tours. Jumpsuits with tassles, with tigers, eagles and sundials, with capes and gigantic belts, there seemed to be no end to the style of attire that Elvis could wear.

With his sad passing in August 1977 the world was robbed of a great entertainer, a great man and a wearer of some of showbiz's greatest ever wardrobes.

Two British Rarities

Most of Elvis' recorded material is now invaluable–the pre-army items in particular are priceless–and amongst this goldmine of material come two items which must surely be Elvis' rarest ever recorded items.

The first is the HMV 45rpm disc *Mystery Train/I Forgot To Remember To Forget.* It was only issued as a 45rpm disc, unlike all the other HMV discs which were issued in both 78 and 45 form. The disc, although made in Great Britain, was issued for overseas markets only, which makes it even harder to locate.

The disc was issued on the standard HMV label and numbered 7MC 42. It is the only British release to duplicate a 'Sun' issue, coupling both sides of Elvis' fifth 'Sun' issue, Sun 223. The British issue also credits 'Scotty and Bill' as does its U.S. counterpart.

From Elvis' rarest 45rpm disc we move now to his rarest 78, and this too is an HMV release, in a roundabout way. The disc in question is the all-talking one known as *The Truth About Me.* It was issued in this country as a 6″ plastic disc and given away free with 'Weekend Mail' in the 1950s. The disc bears a white label with red lettering which reads, "Weekend Mail presents *The Truth About Me,* exclusive, by Elvis Presley, the HMV recording star". Made in England and issued only with 'Weekend Mail' the disc quickly became a collectors' piece. The disc has recently been re-issued on a flexi-disc by the O.E.P.F.C. in 45rpm form. The 78 version however, differs from the new version plus its U.S. counterparts, in that the words RCA Victor have been deleted from the narrative as Elvis' discs were still being issued on the HMV label here in the UK at the time that the disc was first issued.

Is the constant criticism of 'Elvis' movies justified?

There has been continual criticism of Elvis' thirty odd films by critics, by fans and by his fellow stars. Snide remarks in the pop and national press. Has all this been justified? I think not. In this article I am going to consider them in groups.

Pre-Army
"Love Me Tender"
"Loving You"
"Jailhouse Rock"
"King Creole"

His first film, "Love Me Tender" seemed to me to be quite a good first attempt, quite a strong story and Elvis really made an impressive acting début. What on earth the critics meant by saying the cruel and totally untrue things about Elvis and his performance I cannot imagine. It just illustrates the extraordinary effect, preconceived prejudice and fear of something new can have on apparently rational minds.

The great mistake made in this film to my mind was the music, which was totally out of place and did nothing for it and introduced Elvis' "Rock" music totally out of context. I suppose it was inevitable that it should have been pushed in and perhaps fans in those early days would not have accepted a film without it. "Loving You" was rather a routine teen-orientated Rock film. The songs were great of their kind though, and it was interesting to see the early Rock movements.

"Jailhouse Rock" was a much stronger offering. It gave Elvis an opportunity to act. There were some great moments in this film when Elvis really seemed to feel what he was acting. Great Rock music too!

"King Creole" was, in my opinion, one of Elvis' greatest dramatic films. It was very well directed, the story was credible and exciting and it had a good supporting cast. Elvis really was excellent as the boy caught in his underworld environment and struggling against his difficulties. The romantic scenes were most convincing. It was during this film that many fans, and even many critics, began to realize Elvis' real talent as an

by ELIZABETH HARWYSE

actor. The songs were some of the best he has recorded, especially Rock songs.

I would say that the songs, especially the Rock songs in both "Jailhouse Rock" and "King Creole" have never been equalled again in any of his subsequent films.

These films were far better than any of the Rock 'n' Roll type films doing the rounds at that time and Elvis undoubtedly showed far greater acting potential than any of his contemporary Rockers.

Unfortunately, these films had one great drawback from Elvis' point of view. They did present to adults a rather consistent picture of an adolescent rebel, and Elvis tended to be rather too much personally identified with this image.

When he came out of the Army, his management rather went to extremes in the opposite direction so we came to that large section which I will loosely call Glossy Musicals.
"G.I. Blues"
"Blue Hawaii"
"Girls! Girls! Girls!"
"It Happened At The World's Fair"
"Fun In Acapulco"
"Viva Las Vegas"
"Girl Happy"
"Tickle Me"
"Harem Holiday"
"Frankie And Johnnie"
"Paradise, Hawaiian Style"
"California Holiday"
"Easy Come, Easy Go"
"Double Trouble"
"Speedway"
"The Trouble With Girls"

Of these, "G.I. Blues", "Blue Hawaii", "Fun In Acapulco" and "Viva Las Vegas" were what I would call reasonably good family entertainment. Totally escapist, with basically corny stories, but good fun. The songs were well staged and pleasant of their kind. Not great, but very easy listening. "G.I. Blues" was probably the best. I thought Juliet Prowse was by far the best co-star. She is a great dancer and has a strong personality. This was the first Elvis film I had seen and the first time I had seen or heard Elvis. I enjoyed it. I thought Elvis was most charming and amusing and I loved the way he sang.

Now with a lot of hind-sight, I would say that the songs in this film bridged the gap between authentic Rock 'n' Roll and reaching a wider audience. The songs were good of their type and were justly popular at that time. They had plenty of guts and the ballads were charming.

"Blue Hawaii" too had a good selection of songs. Although I do see that they must have been a disappointment to his pre-Army Rock fans, they were most beautifully staged and Elvis was allowed to swing his hips around.

The romantic interest was fairly strong in these films with Elvis concentrating on his female lead. "Girls! Girls! Girls!" was a weaker version of "Blue Hawaii" with less good songs.

"Fun In Acapulco" had great songs. I love Latin American music and I think it suits Elvis' ballad style. Unfortunately, this story was so bitty and confused and the romantic interest so shallow and insipid with Elvis romancing two girls at once and so many repeats of scenes in other films, that what might have been a really good film was only mediocre, and only in the songs and one or two exciting diving scenes was one's attention really engaged.

"It Happened At The World's Fair" was a classic case of the wrong film at the wrong time. This film was really quite passable light entertainment with a slight "Shirley Temple Thirties and all that" air to it. Unfortunately it was released at the height of the Beatles boom. It was quite out of touch with the feeling of the day. The songs were forgettable and not at all in keeping with the kind of music so popular at that time. Critics and many fans alike panned it and it confirmed the young in the view that Elvis was going very square – with some justification. Personally I found bits of it rather appealing, but I did feel that it could have had sharper songs. "Viva Las Vegas" was justly popular, a good, amusing, escapist musical with plenty of go, a good romantic story

and a very personable female lead. The car chase was a classic of its kind and one of the first of these popular features. One thing which always annoys me in connection with this film is the suggestion that Ann-Margret over-shadowed Elvis. This was manifestly rubbish. She was a good foil for him certainly but to suggest that Elvis is so easily over-shadowed is so fatuous that only complete idots or people who have personal or business reasons for saying it could possibly have done so.

I have even read articles which implied that Elvis' advisers have avoided such competition again. If this could conceivably be true they must be out of their minds. Personally I would have thought that it was more likely that the boot was on the other foot and that some female stars, or male stars too for that matter, would hesitate to appear with Elvis in case he over-shadows them.

After "Viva Las Vegas" the standard of the Glossies gradually dropped and total mediocrity set in. Many had their moments but there was too much sameness, too little talent and the songs got into a rut. Too many scenes were repeated. The romantic interest was insipid and there were too many girls, girls, girls, beaches, bar-room brawls, etc. Too many girls pursuing Elvis, with Elvis responding half-heartedly to several girls per picture instead of pursuing a solid relationship with one girl. Whereas in his early films one could believe in his romantic interest. The later films were quite simply a bore with absolutely no acting chances.

The worst of these were "Paradise, Hawaiian Style" and "Harem Holiday", an insult to the intelligence, until they finally scraped the barrel with "The Trouble With Girls". This was completely incoherent and nonsensical and it has resulted in circuits in this country refusing to show Elvis films. No one, not even Elvis can survive this kind of thing.

Of all the Glossies after "Vegas" only one really appealed to me and that was "Clambake". I have to admit to a weakness for this kind of rather corny story and I did think the songs were well staged and quite attractive in their way. Unfortunately, Elvis was very over-weight in this picture. Now I have every sympathy with his struggles with his weight, I have them myself. I also know that with real determination and discipline it can be overcome. For a man in Elvis' position to arrive for a picture in which he is going to play the romantic lead thoroughly over-weight is the height of folly. So sadly this picture was far more of a failure than I think it deserved, because it is not the

sort of thing most men like and romantic young or older women are not going to accept a fat Elvis playing hero. We all know he has lost weight since this picture. It is just unfortunate that at a time when he most needed a good commercial film to help him he chose to appear as he did.

So much for the musicals.

Now for that small group of films which are true comedies. Among these are some of his best post-Army films:

"Follow That Dream"
"Kid Galahad"
"Kissin' Cousins"
"Stay Away, Joe"

Starting with the last and least successful "Stay Away, Joe". Elvis looked really great for this film and it promised something different. I had great hopes for it. Alas, while there were one or two original ideas and comic scenes, these were sandwiched in between very laboured and unfunny ones. The thing I found particularly disappointing was the total lack of a good romantic interest. Elvis, as usual, wasted on a truly terrible girl. But worse than that was the total waste of his opportunities to dance and sing. There were great possibilities for him to do some real Elvis dancing in the party scene. Instead we were given long instrumental passages with very dull girls doing routine movements.

We were promised "U.S. Male", one of his best film songs in years, and it was cut. How stupid can directors get? If a film has musical scenes fans want Elvis singing and particularly Elvis moving about and dancing. They do not want to watch routine show-biz dancing but Elvis doing his own "Thing". This is what it is all about.

So once again all Elvis' talents for dancing, singing, loving and acting are wasted. How sad it is!

"Kissin' Cousins" next. Well I have included this in the comedies because it was rather more rural comedy than glossy musical. This seemed to me to be an unpretentious affair with a fair amount of harmless fun. Really funny sometimes. Elvis looking great and singing well. Pleasant Country and Western songs.

The songs and the film were thoroughly knocked by the British pop press at the time. I consider quite unjustly. This film was a great commercial success and on the whole it deserved to be.

"Kid Galahad" was one of my personal all-time favourites so I cannot be objective about it. I thought it was immensely funny and Elvis played this attractive character with superb restraint. His dry but gentle humour, which always gets me, was very much in evidence. I thought there was a warmth and humour about this character which I found immensely touching. I liked the songs at the time very much but with so many great songs before and since they have paled into insignificance. I found it interesting that this film had quite good reviews in the quality press and not nearly such good ones in the popular dailies.

Finally "Follow That Dream". This film got excellent reviews all round. Justly. It was a really classic comedy and if I was setting out to convert an intelligent friend to Elvis, this is the film I would choose to take him to see. I laughed myself sick almost over it and even to this day when it is some years since I have seen it, I remember little bits and laugh. A beautiful performance. So many so-called comedians bash every point over the head. Elvis just gently nudges it along. I have a sort of feeling that some of the little jokes really went over the heads of some of the less bright cinema-goers.

I have left the three dramatic movies until the last. "Flaming Star", "Wild In The Country" and "Roustabout".

"Roustabout" was almost a glossy and it was the only one which was also a commercial success. Reviews were mixed. I thought it good in parts but like several of Elvis' films it tried to combine comedy and drama and this was not altogether successful. It dragged in places. The trouble was that it was not a very believable story, so that one was not carried away by it. Elvis seemed really to be acting in snippets and although he acted the emotions, anger, love, ruthlessness, etc., very well, one failed to get a coherent character.

"Flaming Star" was an excellent film, exciting and true to life, well acted and with a contemporary theme. So why was it not a commercial success? Well, it had very little box office padding and virtually no songs, so fans who had expected good escapist entertainment did not like it and the kind of cinema-goer who would have appreciated it by and large did not go to see it. It was really a great pity because I am sure that if this film had been a commercial success, it would have opened up a whole new field for Elvis and he would have been offered more exciting and serious roles.

Much the same can be said of "Wild In The Country". Not so good as "Flaming Star" and some scenes were pretty improbable. Also the rebel image was becoming rather tiresome. But there were some really moving love scenes in this – one really believed in them.

The trouble with dramatic films and acting is

that it has to strike some note of reality. The characters have to be totally believable or the audience is bored or it laughs and all is lost. The story in "Wild In The Country" got bogged down in improbable scenes, during which fans and others started losing interest. In comedies, hokum is far easier to brush over.

To sum up, out of the twenty-eight films I have seen, six were very good of their kind. Four were very passable family entertainment, five were absolutely hopeless, silly and boring and the rest pretty mediocre but the real trouble with them was that they were simply rehashes of a basic formula and cinema-goers simply got bored of seeing the same kind of thing every time Elvis was on.

Another big factor in their lack of success was the very mediocre standard of songs. The "Rock" songs becoming increasing routine, uninspired in the singing, in lyric and in melody. Above all they bore no relation to the kind of Rock music that was currently popular with Rock fans. As I understand it, Rock music is of its very nature the "NOW" kind of music. Therefore, anyone choosing to sing this music must always keep within the framework and feeling for what is currently the trend. The tempo must be right, the backing up-to-date and the overall sound must relate to contemporary taste or it must try to create a new sound. Jogging along with a dated format simply will not do.

It is noticeable that Elvis' recent album and releases have achieved this necessary formula.

It is difficult to assess Elvis' acting potential. Certainly in some scenes he has shown great possibilities, but it has always seemed to me that he acts emotion but not character. This may well be because most characters in his films tend to be not very distinctive. Certainly he has a flair for comedy but I do wonder how he could cope with a character basically opposed to his own.

What would I like to see him do in the future?

Well, he has done one thing that I have always longed for him to do and that is film his stage act.

I am not against the glossy musicals at their best. I thought them very entertaining, but I do want a good story, carefully chosen contemporary songs and above all Elvis moving in his own inimitable way and one good female star.

I would like to seem him choosing at least one good dramatic part and giving it a real try, even if this involves starting with another big-name actor and even playing second fiddle if it would mean seeing him in a better film.

Finally, I agree with, I think it was Wayne Stierle, who said he should make a film of his own story. This surely would be the ultimate in Presley films.

"Elvis, That's The Way It Is" goes part of the way towards meeting this need, but a film showing much more of the Elvis Story would be welcomed by every fan and probably a large section of the general public.

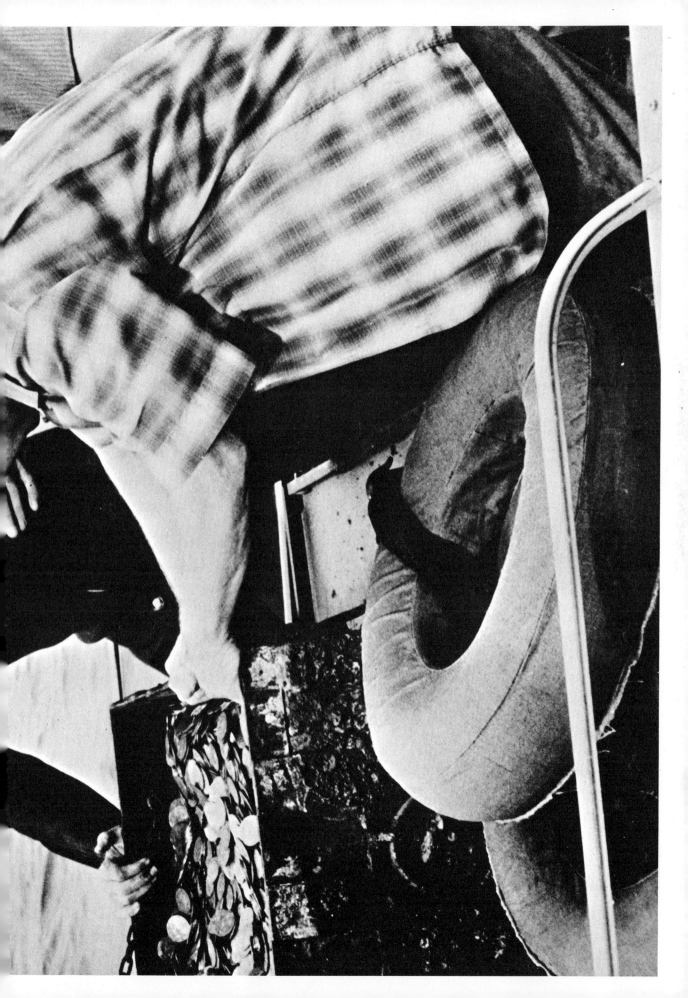

The World's GREATEST Showman

by Anne E. Nixon

I have seen many "live" Elvis performances, and several Elvis "moods". Sometimes he's serious and singing hard and strong; sometimes he has the "sillies", as Tom Diskin calls them, and breaks up laughing throughout the show; sometimes he's in an infectiously happy mood, and sometimes he's a little uptight. Elvis never attempts to cover up his moods, and the audience invariably gets caught up in whatever mood he's in. There is one particular show that stands out in my memory, that combined many of Elvis' moods; an absolutely rivetting show that anyone who saw it could never forget. From beginning to end it underlined the supreme showmanship that is Elvis Presley. Let's relive this superb performance, Elvis' closing show in Las Vegas on 3 September 1973. First of all, though, a flashback to the 3 am show on Sunday, 2 September, when Elvis startled us by coming onstage riding on Lamar Fike's back, and, when he'd stopped laughing, asked, "How can you top that entrance, man?"!

The closing show crowd was excited, and waited impatiently through "2001", anticipating Elvis' entrance. He surprised us all again. Out came Lamar Fike, a mountain of a man, carrying the king on his back, but on Elvis' back was a monkey! The brown-and-white stuffed toy was taped to Elvis' shoulders, its arms around his neck. The astonished audience watched as Lamar carried on right across the stage, then came back centre-stage and set Elvis down. Elvis was laughing as he took his guitar from Charlie Hodge, but he couldn't manage the guitar very well with the monkey on his back. He began "C.C. Rider", with a few lyric changes, with reference to the monkey, and threw in a "Hang on, Kid!" at one point. The audience was in disarray, laughing at Elvis' facial expressions. He said, before singing "I Got A Woman": "Good evening, ladies and gentlemen, I brought one of my relatives with me." More lyric changes in Elvis' second number: "I got a monkey, way across town," and so on. Someone yelled out, "Give him a kiss, Elvis," as Elvis was sinking down to JD's low bass note in "Amen". Looking back at the monkey, Elvis thrust the microphone near its mouth, and said, "He's an ape, that ain't no monkey." He began "Love me", but didn't

move along the front row as usual to accept kisses and give out scarves. He stood centre-stage, and although he laughed a little during much of the song he sang quite seriously, almost making us believe he'd forgotten the monkey. At the end of the song, Charlie unstuck the toy for him, and it sat onstage for the rest of the show.

Elvis did a fine version of "Steamroller Blues", followed by a strong "Lord, You Gave Me A Mountain". The show's mood had changed, as Elvis' mood became serious. "Trouble" followed, and Elvis pounded out his rock medley of "Flip, Flop, Fly", etc. At the close of "Hound Dog", he began a "Ch Ch Ch" kind of sound. It went on and on, as he continued to improvise. The band behind him picked it up, and jammed along. Elvis was bent over double, knees bent, and moving from side to side, real gone! The audience was half hypnotised, half screaming. The crowd of

Scottish fans at my table were all screaming—it was a tremendous atmosphere. We applauded, feeling wrung out.

"Elvis, I want your scarf," called a feller down front. "OK, you can have it . . . here you are," and the king passed down his flame-red scarf to the upstretched hand. The fans nearby crowded in on Elvis, and handed him up a Summer Festival Boater. He wore it for a moment and did a soft shoe shuffle. He walked back centre-stage; his serious mood became a "sillies" mood, as on the way he kicked over a music stand near to Charlie. "I'd like to sing a little bit of 'Love Me Tender' for you. 'Love me tender, love me true'," he squeaked in a high voice, very rapidly. "That's a little bit of 'Love Me Tender', speeded up!" He turned to Charlie and urged quietly: "Put a scarf on—*do it!*" As the introduction began, Elvis fell flat onto the stage, and began to sing, and Charlie walked over to him and draped white scarves over his face. He adlibbed a verse: "Adios a madre, bye bye poppa too, to Hell with the Hilton Hotel,"—the many British fans present cheered, and the last line was lost on the audience, due to the cheers—"Priscilla, too!" More adlibbing in the same song: "I will help you all I can, because I know you're blind." Elvis was back on his feet, as we applauded. His jibe at the Hilton was unexpected, but welcome to the British fans, whose reservations the hotel had tried to cancel that season, and we felt that he was on our side.

A ripple of excitement ran through the audience as "Fever" began. Elvis stood out on the ramp, the spotlight picking out the multi-coloured stones on his white jumpsuit. His silly mood continued, as he adlibbed a verse about J. D. Sumner and Myrna Smith of the Sweet Inspirations. After the line, "I light up when you call my name," he mimicked the fans, by shouting "Elvis" in a high voice. He continued to adlib until the end of the song, throwing in lines like, "I'm allergic to cats," and "Fahrenheit or Siamese," and telling his shaking legs to, "Cool it, you fools!" Quite the best "crazy" version of "Fever" I've ever heard him do.

The lights stayed off at the end of the song for a few seconds longer than usual. From our table in the centre of the showroom, we could detect something large and white moving across the stage. The lights came on again to reveal—a BED! The audience, already in a state of disarray, went wild! Elvis fell flat onto the bed, and commenced singing "What Now My Love". He turned onto his side, and thumped the pillow, saying in a high squeaky voice, "Where's she gone, where's she gone?" Halfway through the song, Elvis got off the bed, and we applauded as it was rolled offstage. Elvis continued the song, in a remarkably controlled voice. The audience, however, couldn't stop laughing, and for those of us who witnessed that amazing scene, Elvis had ruined forever the "seriousness" of "What Now, My Love"; we'd evermore giggle on hearing that song.

The "Suspicious Minds" introduction began, but Elvis started to sing "Bridge Over Troubled Water", fighting it out with the orchestra, but giving up after a couple of verses. "Hold it, hold it, hold it—hold the show! Just drop everything, everybody fall out!" Charlie Hodge dramatically fell over. Elvis walked over to him, to say, "Bless you, son!" He apologised to us: "I don't really like to do that, but I gotta stick to one song or the other. Let's do 'Bridge Over Troubled Water'." He fooled around with the lyrics at the start of the tune. Someone called out to interrupt him. "Shut up," intoned Elvis in a deep voice, and the audience's laughter, and the smattering of applause at this, made Elvis forget the words of the song. He stopped singing, and the band took over. They stood up, and sang in unison, and the audience joined in, as Elvis stood, listening. "Oh, that's nice—listen, listen, the Ted Mack Amateur Hour! Very nice. Thank you very much," said Elvis. The band sat down, and Elvis finished the song, giving it a powerful rendition. Afterwards, he thanked the band for helping out. A good version of "Suspicious Minds" followed, with a few adlibs thrown in, and then Elvis began his introductions. He paused as Charlie began to pick up the sheet music he'd kicked over earlier. "Charlie, you don't have to do that, get someone to come out here, somebody backstage come out and pick the sheet music up. Joe, Sonny, Red, Lamar . . ." Sonny West and Red West appeared and picked up the sheet music. Elvis, satisfied, got on with the introductions. "OK. Over on the left is Mr. J. D. Sumner and the Stumps—Stamps Quartet. The young ladies up front are the Sweet something-or-other—the Sweet Inspirations. The little girl that does our high-voiced singing is Cathy Westmoreland. On the lead guitar," he said in a deep voice, "is James Burton. On the rhythm guitar is John *Wilkinson*," he emphasised the name, having got it wrong so many times before. In a deep drawl he said, "And on the drums is Ronnie Tutt." So the introductions continued, 'til Elvis came to Joe Guercio. "Put that light back on Joe, please. Would you look at that belt! Stand up, Joe, please. It's fantastic!"

The usual personalities were in the audience, including actor George Hamilton, Col. Parker, and singer Bobbie Gentry. Elvis enthused over her: "She's opening at the Frontier. Go and see her act, she's a wow!" He introduced his dad, who came onstage, arms raised, to great cheers. Elvis walked to the front of the stage, to the corner seat between the ramp and the stage, and leant down. "I want you to say hello to Linda, she's a friend. Hello, dear!" And he raised Linda Thompson's arm. The audience applauded—albeit politely—obviously realising who Linda was.

"I'd like to sing a song that I hope you like." A fan yelled out. "Hey, wait a minute now, I'm running this show! I'd like to sing a song that was done by, er, what's-'is-name"—Elvis couldn't bring Richard Harris's name to mind—"It's a great song called, 'My boy'." So beautifully did Elvis sing this song, it was a joy to listen to him. "It's a good song," he told us. "I've saved Charlie Hodge 'til the last, because he's the least! No—because he does this fantastic harmony with me. He's been doing it for thirteen years, and he does it so well, that it's almost like one voice." And Elvis paid tribute to a somewhat over-looked group member. Elvis' next song was "I Can't Stop Loving You", ending with his usual incredible voice-bending notes. At the start of "American Trilogy" he sang, "look away, Disneyland," and urged the Stamps to: "Sing it, fellas, sing it now, *do* it!" And he emphasised the word "Disneyland" in their solo verse of the song. Elvis sang the remainder of the song completely seriously, a marvellous rendition of one of the finest tunes he's ever sung onstage. Oh, what a wonderful moment it was when the flute solo had been played, and the music began to build! The look on Elvis' face was one of total involvement. The applause reflected the audience's appreciation.

Having created a mood of musical perfection, the king launched into "A Big Hunk Of Love", a foot-stomping tune that took us back to the early rockin' days. He took time to tell us, afterwards: "I'd like to say something about the song that we did before, 'American Trilogy'. The guy that plays the flute solo, Jimmy Mullidore, he's played it 144 times and never missed a note. Thank you—stand up, Jimmy. The trumpet players, they've actually split their lips blowing so hard, really. We kid a lot, and have a lot of fun, but we really love to sing and play music and entertain people. That's the name of the game!" As the applause died down, Elvis said, "I'd like to do a song that's one of my favourites, and I hope you like it." His version of "The First Time Ever I Saw Your Face" was tenderly and beautifully interpreted, so much better than his recorded version—but then, most of his "live" songs are.

"This chain that I've got round my neck," he indicated the heavy gold chain, "was given to me last night by the hotel, the Hilton Hotel. It has my initials here, and it's just a favour for doing a third show last night." He hesitated for a moment, and his face became serious. "There's a guy here, that works in the Italian restaurant, his name's Mario"—a smattering of applause—"and these people are getting ready to fire him as soon as I leave, and I don't want him to go, 'cos he needs a job, and I think the Hilton's bigger 'n that." We applauded, a little surprised at Elvis' words. "No disrespect," he concluded, "but just wake up Conrad and tell him about Mario's job, that's all." He began "Mystery Train", singing it very forcefully, then, as the tune changed to "Tiger Man" Elvis interrupted his musicians to say: "This next song is dedicated to the hierarchy and the staff of the Hilton Hotel." And the king of

the Vegas jungle sang "Tiger Man" fiercely.

"How Great Thou Art" is the finest song I've heard Elvis do "live", and this was his next selection. Elvis put so much power and sincerity into his singing, that the whole showroom vibrated and you thought the balcony must surely come falling down. This is one song that Elvis *never* fools around in. As Elvis ended on his high note, he flung back his arm, and a shower of sweat from his face was beaded in the spotlight. "... Do it again?" he asked. "Yeah!" we encouraged. He repeated the end of the song. "Do it *again*? I don't care, I'll sing it all night!" He repeated the final verse again, so obviously enjoying himself. "You're very nice," he thanked us.

To our surprise, he began softly singing "Help Me Make It Through The Night", afterwards asking Charlie to bring his chair onstage. Elvis sat down on the blue chair, and tilted his head backward, a look of exhaustion for a moment on his face. "I'd like to tell you a little story." His voice was quiet and intensely serious. No-one knew what he was going to say; we sat still, expectantly. "There was a man in Florida, he was dying of cancer and he was in a coma; he'd been in a coma for three days, and his wife was sitting up by his side, and on the third morning she lay down beside him and dozed off to sleep, and he felt her as she dozed off to sleep, and at the same time he felt himself starting to die..." The audience was gazing, hypnotised, awestruck, in silence, at the lone figure seated in the spotlight; it was as though a spell had been cast on us.

Elvis continued: "And he took his notepad from beside the bed, and he wrote, 'Softly as I leave you, long before your arms can beg me stay, for one more hour, for one more day'..." The orchestra had picked up the song, and were playing almost imperceptibly behind Elvis as he spoke the poignant words of this true story: "After all the years, I can't bear the tears to fall, so, softly, softly, I will leave you... there." His voice had become almost a whisper. "That's all, take it home," he told his musicians, barely waiting for our applause. It took a few moments for us to come out of the spell he'd cast. Then the whole audience stood up, as he sang "Can't Help Falling In Love". He was distributing white scarves as on a conveyor belt, fed by Charlie. At the song's conclusion, he came forward on the ramp. The audience was cheering. Lamar Fike appeared, and Elvis jumped onto his broad back and rode away offstage, then came back on his own two feet, to the delight of the still wildly applauding crowd. The gold curtain went back up, and Elvis came down the ramp again, giving out scarves and shaking hands. At length, he turned and ran offstage, his hand rippling the inside of the blue curtain, and he was gone.

The mind-blown audience was left to go its separate ways, having been fortunate enough to witness a superlative and inspired performance by Elvis, the world's greatest showman.

ANNE E. NIXON

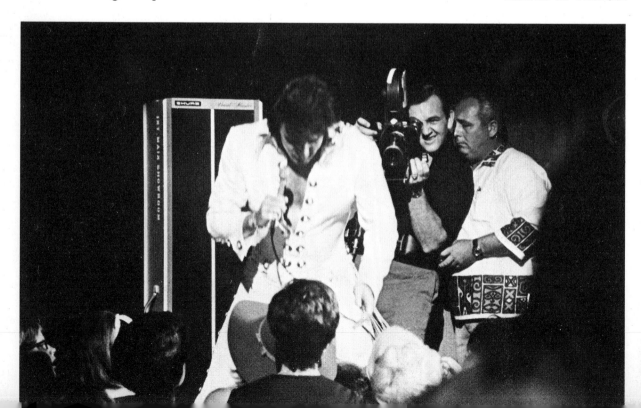

The man behind the music of ELVIS

by Peter Jones

Behind every top star is a top manager. Colonel Tom Parker in the case of Elvis Presley – a backroom presiding genius whose name is known to millions of fans the world over.

But behind every top singing star there is usually a top music publisher. The man who copes with the vast amount of lyrics and melodies that come tumbling through the letter-box just about every day of the week.

The man behind Elvis Presley in this respect is one Freddy Bienstock, a Swiss-born charmer with a fantastic knowledge of the pop music industry – one of the shrewdest judges of a song in the business.

Freddy looks after Elvis' publishing interests and has been involved since the second Presley recording session for R.C.A. Victor. And, like so many of the employees or partners on the Presley scene, he is a one hundred per cent FAN!

Says Freddy: "Elvis is quite simply a natural charisma." And to save you looking up the dictionary, may I say that the definition of charisma is: "An extraordinarily high degree of artistic genius."

So Freddy has a specialist knowledge of what makes Elvis tick. He told me on one of his regular visits to London: "Where Elvis scores is that he has a remarkable memory for a song. I've tried to trick him on several occasions. Say I'd presented him with a song – one I liked. Maybe he'd say that he didn't think it was right for him at that particular time. Okay, I'd accept his word on the matter and forget it.

"Maybe a few years would pass. Then I'd remember that song and decide to try it again with Elvis. He'd listen. Then, half-way through, turn to me with that special smile of his. "You played me that way back," he'd say, "you can't fool me." And the truth is that I couldn't.

"For years I was El's sort of A and R man – artist and repertoire – only I was dealing most with just him. I collected the material together – it all went through me – for more than twelve years. But in the end, it was up to Elvis. He made the final decision.

"Back in those days, when Hill and Range was El's publishing outlet, we had quite a few writers under contract just to us. So I'd call them in and tell them we wanted a new song for Elvis. They'd know the sort of thing we wanted. There were guys like Doc Pomus, Otis Blackwell, Mort Shuman, Sid Tepper and Roy Bennett – oh, and Joe Byars down in Nashville.

"But that wasn't the end of it. We'd get literally hundreds of songs, unsolicited, through the post every week – and I'd become a sort of clearinghouse. Now the thing with Elvis was that he never did get too deep into the writing scene. He knew the sort of thing that suited him, but he lacked a certain something.

"Tell you what – I'd say that certain something was a real pride in authorship. He'd write his songs and then show them to me, but he'd never kind of fight for them. He'd never let himself be influenced by the fact that he'd written them – they'd just go into the pile with all the other possible songs. He could have done it easily by this time in his career. You know, insisted that we used his own songs and let the other writers go hang.

"It was a fascinating time in my own career, just watching the quite astonishing grasp that Elvis had on the music business.

"Still, Elvis wrote only a handful of songs. If he was dissatisfied with certain lines, he'd make some changes . . . that's in other peoples' songs. And after

that, later on, he just made suggestions to writers rather than get personally involved.

"And there was the film side of things. People wrote the scripts but we had to have the widest possible selection of songs. So we'd give out dozens and dozens of the copies of the film scripts. We'd just mark in places where the songs had to go into the action. We gave the writers a free hand – they could produce material for each song-break if they wanted. That way we almost always had four or five songs for each spot in the movie . . . and again Elvis would have the biggest possible choice. We'd get the songs in on demonstration records – that made it easier for Elvis to pick out the winner."

The sheer enthusiasm for Elvis Presley shows through in everything Freddy Bienstock says. He said: "You've just got to see him working live to get the full impact. In films, on records – he's dynamic. But the real Presley comes through when he's there in the flesh. He's two men, really. He honestly is two men.

"There's the on-stage Presley, the tremendous performer. And there's the off-stage man who speaks very quietly, is always polite, and who is almost constantly worrying about his weight.

"I'd say he gets upset easily by criticism, even after all these years. He reads the stories of fans all round the world wanting to see him. He knows he can't do everything. And in that kind of matter, the Colonel is in charge.

"Now the Colonel is a very close friend of mine. He has this kind of paternal relationship with Elvis. He's a fantastic practical joker, though when you get him on a business matter, he can be hard as nails. The Colonel has remarkable loyalty towards his friends – though I admit he doesn't make friends all that easily. Once you're 'in', though, he'll stick with you through thick and thin.

"But when you talk about Elvis, you have to mention his personal courage. There was the courage in facing all the early criticism. The courage he needed to make a real go of being a full-time soldier. And the courage he called upon when he made that cabaret appearance at the International in Las Vegas after a gap of some nine years."

Freddy Bienstock thinks there can never be a night to match that particular opening. Elvis had said: "I got tired of singing to the guys I beat up in the motion pictures." The opening was, as is history now, organized with a sort of military attention to detail . . . the build-up of the band, the enlistment of The Sweet Inspirations and The Imperials and so on. How Elvis had insisted on three full dress rehearsals that very afternoon.

Even Elvis was nervous as the build-up to the show moved relentlessly along. But listen to Freddy Bienstock for his summary.

"That was no ordinary opening night. It was Elvis – and that meant more big names there than ever before – and a much greater call on the artist's courage. Elvis went magnificently. I remember Burt Bacharach telling me afterwards that he'd clapped so hard he'd got blisters on his hands. Fantastic. But then I've never known Elvis to be less than fantastic."

As I was saying, the publisher behind Elvis the star is as much a fan as the rest of us.

Remember that bit about "charisma – an extraordinarily high degree of artistic genius"? It's right, you know.

☆☆☆☆☆☆☆☆☆☆☆☆☆☆☆☆☆☆
ELVIS said......
☆☆☆☆☆☆☆☆☆☆☆☆☆☆☆☆☆☆

Since Elvis never gives interviews now, and rarely gives press conferences, his on-stage chat is almost the only time that fans have an opportunity to hear him talk, and to savour his great sense of humour. The following comments, ad-libs, and anecdotes are among the most interesting and amusing he said during his last three summer seasons in Las Vegas. So sit back, and enjoy reading what Elvis said.

After singing "Polk Salad Annie": At least that woke me up! I'd like to welcome you to the International Hilton, Hawaiian Village, Kahala Motel, Inn . . . My name's all out front, on the bathroom, ceiling, floor . . .!

(Midnight show, 2–9–72)

Acknowledging the British fans' block booking: I'd like to acknowledge the presence of somebody in the audience. There's a fan club that came all the way from England here tonight; there's 200–250 of 'em here. I hope you enjoy the show, thank you for coming over.

(Dinner show, 4–9–72)

After J. D. Sumner had sung "Walk That Lonesome Road" in his deep voice: I can't even think that low!

(Closing show, 4–9–72)

To Bill Porter, his sound engineer: This microphone don't sound as good as the one I had last night. I'm quittin'! It's not your fault, Bill, you're a nice guy—just jump off the balcony! *Elvis put two microphones to his ears as in "That's The Way It Is" and said:* Hello, hello? *Later, realising the band couldn't hear him properly he told them:* It'd be a lot better if you guys could hear me back there. It's not your fault, it's the microphone. You can't do the whole show by instinct alone, you've got to know what song I'm gonna

sing. I may sing Walt Disney's, "Talk To The Animals"! *Then, referring again to the microphones, he changed the words of "Suspicious Minds" to:* Let's don't let a good sound die, we had it for 3½ weeks, oh God, what happend to it?

(Dinner show, 30–8–73)

A lady called out, "What about us ladies over 30?": Ladies over 30? What about you, honey? I've never thought about it one way or the other. *Two songs later, after clearing his throat loudly, he added:* Wait a minute, now! People's voices change when they get to a certain age, don't they Ronnie? Over 30!

(Dinner show, 30–8–73)

Commenting on his black jumpsuit: I usually dress all in white, because this room's hot, so if I just melt during the show, folks!

(Dinner show, 31–8–73)

by ANNE E. NIXON

After singing "Fever". That song's a lot of fun to do. I can hardly keep my breakfast down! In Las Vegas, you go backwards, you have breakfast in the evenings, and after you've been here a month, you don't know where, when, what, who . . . or why!

(Dinner show, 31–8–73)

Introducing Lisa: I'd like to do a song for my little daughter, she's been here for about 4 nights. Stand up, Lisa. She's 5 years old. Turn round honey, turn the other way. It's a big room. That's enough, don't take it away from daddy!

(Dinner show, 30–8–73)

Sharing his groups' generosity with us: The Sweet Inspirations went over to the Jerry Lewis Telethon today, and The Stamps went over to the hospital to sing some songs to the patients. And I went out and rode a wild buffalo! *(Modestly, he omitted to mention that he too had gone over to the Telethon at the Sahara hotel and given $10,000.)*

(Dinner show, 2–9–73)

For the closing show in September, 1973, Elvis came onstage with a stuffed monkey attached to his back. During the first 3 songs, he made these comments: I brought one of my relatives with me. Good evening, ladies and gentlemen and animal lovers. I'm gonna sing some songs, walk around, and try to get this monkey off my back. If he wants to go to the bathroom, I'm in trouble!

(Closing show, 3–9–73)

He adlibbed a verse of "Fever": "Myrna Smith and J. D. Sumner, had a very mad affair, when their wives and husbands caught them, saw nothin' but teeth and hair!" *Onstage, Myrna, J. D., and the groups were cracked up with laughter.*

(Closing show, 3–9–73)

On his bout of 'flu: I had a cold one day this week, and I had to quit, had to miss two shows, that's all, I missed two shows. This one night I had a temperature and they wouldn't let me go on, 'cause with a temperature you lose your equilibrium, your balance and so forth. But in the whole 19 years I've only missed about 6/7 shows.

(Midnight show, 30–8–74)

After a fan gave him a huge stuffed tiger with a karate jacket and belt on: This thing here is cute. My little daughter is coming in this weekend, she's 6 years old. If you don't mind I'll give it to her, OK? She would love that. What did you do, did you have it made? You made it? You decorated it? That's beautiful, it really is . . . then people wonder why I don't want to miss a show. I love it out here. I know that people come from all over, they fly, they drive here, and there's not anyone on this stage, I mean anybody, that had rather be here than anywhere else in the world.

(Midnight show, 30–8–74)

To the people in the balcony: It's good to see you, but the view from up there—is it OK? 'Cause I went up to watch Barbra Streisand, and she looked like a midget, got this big voice and little bitty body.

(Dinner show, 31–8–74)

Talking about Lisa: She's really a well-adjusted little child, she's just turned 6 years' old. The only thing is, she calls me "Ailvis"! I say, "Honey, don't do that". I don't really like my name anyway, when I was younger I used to try and get everyone to call me Aron, that's my middle name. 'Cause I had a twin brother, his middle name was Garon. I liked that. I didn't like Elvis. Aron—I tried to get everyone to call me that but, no, Elvy—Elvis, whatever! Lisa, my daughter: "Where you goin', Ailvis?" "Honey, I'm your father, your daddy." "Can I go with you, Ailvis?"

(Midnight show, 31–8–74)

Introducing John Bassey, from the Memphis Football Team, who were all in the audience: I was at a football game in Memphis, I'm in his box. They put me a closed-circuit television in, not him. He saw me halfway through the game and said, "How come you've got a television?" I said, "It's who you know, John!" For the second half, his blood pressure had to be 900 degrees. I said, "John, you've got to settle down, your heart'll roll out of your shoe!" So, for the second half, we stacked a chair up, and put the television so that he could see the instant replay.

(Midnight show, 31–8–74)

Explaining about his swollen right hand: I was working out in karate, giving a demonstration in board breaking techniques. I can break a brick, so that happens occasionally. There's nothing broken there, it's just swollen up. I was giving a demonstration for some people coming to visit. I did a movie called "G.I. Blues". At that particular time I was a first degree black belt. I did this movie, "G.I. Blues", and we were working out in-between takes. We were doing board breaking, and tiles and bricks, and so on, demonstrating, showing-off, and I blocked a kick the wrong way, so this happened, this came up the same way. Except I was in the middle of a movie with Juliet Prowse. I do a love scene with a guitar, and there was this big fat hand. Nothing they could do. They tried to put make-up on it, it looked like it belonged to another person. It was black. It came out on the album—look at the album, "G.I. Blues", sometimes, look at that hand. Looks like somebody blew it up!

(Dinner show, 1–9–74)

Telling us about the statue of an Elizabethan lady on the showroom wall, that he painted: I've never liked the way this showroom's looked, the interior decorating. It's too wide for a performer. I had this ramp made so I could come out a little closer to the audience. Put a spotlight on the statues on that wall. It's OK, it's nice—I don't know what it is, but it's nice! Tom Jones was in the other night, and he's from Wales, wherever, Wales, Mississippi! I asked Tom what it was, and he said it was King Edward? King George—excuse me, your Majesty! Take the spotlight up and put it on those angels. Look at those dudes, boy! Big fat angels! Put the spotlight on this wall over here. You will notice a slight difference, those of the Caucasian race. That's what it is, isn't it? Caucasion? It was on my army draft card. Anyway, the other night I came down here about 4.30 in the morning, and a couple of friends of mine, who work for me—Jerry Schilling and Red West—Red wrote "Separate Ways", he

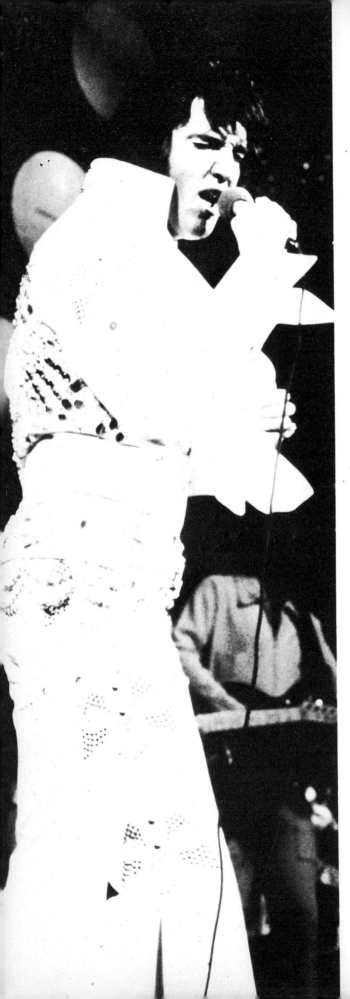

wrote "Why Can't Every Day Be Like Christmas", he wrote, "If You Talk In Your Sleep". Red is a 2nd degree black belt in Karate, he has a school in Memphis, and I'm very proud of him. Anyway, he climbed the fence where they keep all the supplies, paint, and so forth, he climbed a fence as high as this curtain (*meaning the 20 ft high stage curtains*). He went down, got a little can of black paint, put it on his belt, came back, climbed over, and we went over there and we stacked two tables up. I got up with the paint and a brush, and I was Michealangelo, or the guy that painted the ceiling in the Vatican, whatever —the Sistine Chapel? Is that it? Sistine—that was his girlfriend! Sistine. No, I'm only kidding. Anyway, I painted that statue, it took me 30 minutes to do. The hotel haven't said a word, but I just thought I'd share it with you.

(Dinner show, 1–9–74)

Asking Charlie for a drink: Give me some water, my mouth feels like Bob Dylan slept in it!

(Dinner show, 1–9–74)

He was wearing a black suit, walking onto the ramp in the darkness of the start of "Fever": Phew, it's dark up here . . . if I get lost, in this black suit they'll never find me!

(Midnight show, 1–9–74)

Showing us his rings, just before the end of the show: See this ring (*a huge one on his left hand*) I wore this thing in that Aloha Special from Hawaii. A lot of people thought it was one solid big diamond. No, it's a 1½ carat diamond, and there are some 16 carat diamonds all round it. It's the biggest diamond I've ever seen. It was my Xmas gift to myself! I just thought I deserved it! This one I have here (*on his right hand*) I had this designed for the stage. It has oval-shaped, pear-shaped diamonds. This here (*again on his right hand*) a Japanese lady gave me. Are you here, dear? Stand up. Put that spotlight on her, she came from Japan. Tonight, between shows she gave me this ring. Honey, what is the stone in the middle? A blue star sapphire with diamonds. Thank you, thank you.

(Midnight show, 1–9–74)

Talking about the Telethon in Las Vegas, being held over Labor Day weekend, he was reminded of a story about Jerry Lewis, the Telethon host: When I first got out of the army in 1960, I bought a Rolls Royce. I was driving in Beverley Hills one day and Jerry Lewis pulled up beside me. He looked over at me. (*Elvis turned his head slowly to the side to show the expression that had*

been on Jerry's face) I did the same thing. (*Elvis turned his head again and repeated the expression*) He called my manager the same day, and said, "Tell Elvis not to drive a Rolls Royce without a tie on." I swear to God! Well, I will give you a couple of guesses to the message I sent back!

(Dinner show, Labor Day, 2–9–74)

Introducing himself: Good evening, ladies and gentlemen, my name is Tom Jones, you went to the wrong place . . . no, I hope you have a good time this evening; my name is really Charlton Heston, I parted the Red Sea!

(Dinner show, 2–9–74)

As Elvis began "Fever", Priscilla, in the centre front booth, yelled out, "Sing it!" Elvis stopped singing, and laughed, then said: Hold it a minute! My ex-wife is in the audience yelling (*and he imitated her high voice*) "Sing it Honey, sing it honey!"

(Dinner show, 2–9–74)

The introduction to "Hound Dog": I was on the Steve Allen show, and I was . . . (*he imitated the way he moved on that TV show in 1956*) I was just doing it in time with the music. I wasn't doing any obscene moves, really. They put me on TV and they filmed me from the waist up. Steve Allen had me on his show. At that time, Steve Allen, when I did the show, he outrated the Ed Sullivan show. Ed sent Steve a telegram that said, "You Rat!" Anyway, Steve's got a weird mind. He's a funny, funny man, believe me, he's a brilliant genius when it comes to comedy. He had me dressed in a tuxedo and tails, singing to this little fat hound dog on a stool. Not moving a muscle, I had to sing to this little fat dog, "You ain't nuthin' but a hound . . ." The whole song I didn't move a muscle. Steve Allen did that. I love him for it, but I'll never forgive him!

(Dinner show, 2–9–74)

Introducing Priscilla: My ex-wife is right here. Priscilla, stand up, and let them see you, come on . . . (*she does, to big applause*). She's beautiful. Hold little Lisa up, hold Lisa up . . . turn around. (*Lisa stands up in the booth, to more applause.*)

(Dinner show, 2–9–74)

Introducing celebrities: The feller that I was kidding you about earlier, Steve Allen. One of the funniest men around, and he's a good friend of mine, and he's really out of sight! Steve Allen . . . (*applause*). There's another gentleman in the audience who's a very distinguished actor, and

I met this man at Paramount Studios. I was about 23 years old. He was doing the "Ten Commandments" at the time, and he was walking around dressed as Moses. He'd come into the dining room when I was eating, and there I was, just come out of Memphis, Tennessee: "There's Moses!" . . . Charlton Heston. (*Big applause*). Boy, he's made some dillys hasn't he? "Ben-Hur"—whooo! Lord have Mercy! I'll never forget that in my life, when he came off that mountain, from Mount Sinai, remember? He had those tablets and that white hair. I'd like to talk to him sometime and ask him what kind of a state of mind he had to get into, to do that part. Can you imagine that? He'd just talked to God, and he came down the mountainside with those tablets under his arm, white hair. I'd like to ask him how he got his mind thinkin' the part. Phew! It's tougher than a nickel stovepipe.

(Dinner show, 2–9–74)

Elvis had to go off-stage for a couple of minutes. First, he said to The Stamps: I'd like to ask The Stamps to leave the stage . . . to do one of my favourite songs, "Why Me Lord?" *Elvis then disappeared, and came back as the song ended, to ask:* What'd I miss? OK—these suits—if you have to go to the bathroom (*much audience laughter*) they're in one piece, you know. In fact, Priscilla designed these things. Woman! Female! But they're all in one piece, you got to . . . (*he demonstrated how he had to pull the suit off his shoulders*). So, nowhere to go, you gotta run!

(Dinner show, 2–9–74)

When a Scots lad gave him a tammy hat, he put it on, then joked: Oh boy, I'm glad he didn't bring me one of those kilts!

(Dinner show, 2–9–74)

Introducing himself: Good evening, ladies and gentlemen, my name is Bill Cosby . . . er, Elvis closed last night. I'm a little lighter skinned than you thought I was!

(Closing show, Midnight, 2–9–74)

Noticing an old friend in the audience: See this younglady right here? Her name is Judy Spreckles. Let me tell you a story about her. I came to Hollywood, I was 20 years old, to do "Love Me Tender". Her family was the Spreckles sugar family—you've heard of it, haven't you? Yeah, well, I guess everybody has, because it's a big company. She gave me a four black star sapphire ring, that I kept up until Priscilla and I were married, and Priscilla used it as an engagement ring.

(Midnight show, 2–9–74)

Introducing Vicki Carr: There's a lady in the audience, she's been in to see my show twice before. The reason we have a mutual respect is because the only way we know how to sing a song is from the gut—out, both of us. You know who I'm talking about? Her name is Vicki Carr.

(Midnight show, 2–9–74)

Acknowledging the tremendous ovation after singing "It's Now Or Never": I couldn't have a better audience if I'd stood outside and paid everybody twenty dollars to come in here. You are out of sight!

(Midnight show, 2–9–74)

Before singing "Can't Help Falling In Love", to end the show, and the Summer Season, Elvis spoke about his rings again, and concluded: The reason I'm telling you this is, you helped pay for 'em!

(Midnight show, 2–9–74)

So, that's what Elvis said. These snippets demonstrate his skill at ad-libbing, his humility, and most of all, his tremendous sense of humour. I hope you enjoyed hearing what Elvis said.

Pencil sketch by Michael Pearce

HISTORY OF THE ELVIS LP COVER

COMPILED BY MARTIN BLOYE

Elvis Presley's records were first issued in Great Britain on the HMV label (the HMV catalogue being deleted in 1958). During 1957 his records were also issued on the RCA label, records being pressed and distributed through Decca Record Company. In 1968, however, RCA themselves took over full control of the pressing and distribution of Elvis' discs in Great Britain.

As a result of these changes to distributors of Elvis' records many of his earlier LPs have been deleted. When some of these were re-released later there occurred many changes in LP cover design and also song tracks. It is these changes that I propose to examine in the following article where of particular interest I have referred to equivalent American LPs.

1. ROCK 'N' ROLL NO. 1—HMV (CLP 1093)

BLUE SUEDE SHOES: I GOT A SWEETIE (WOMAN): I'M COUNTING ON YOU: I'M LEFT, YOU'RE RIGHT, SHE'S GONE: THAT'S ALL RIGHT (MAMA): MONEY HONEY: MYSTERY TRAIN: I'M GONNA SIT RIGHT DOWN AND CRY: TRYIN' TO GET TO YOU: ONE-SIDED LOVE AFFAIR: LAWDY MISS CLAWDY: SHAKE RATTLE AND ROLL.

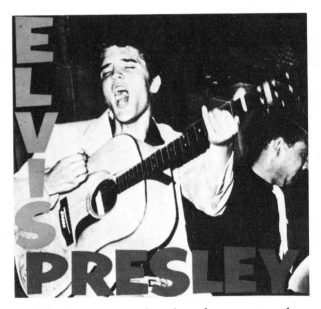

Issued in November 1956 and Elvis' very first LP release in Britain, the cover shows Elvis, in a black-and-white photograph, wearing a white suit and playing his guitar. Running down the side of the album cover is "Elvis" in large pink letters and across the bottom "Presley" in large green letters. The reverse side of cover has extensive sleeve notes by Bob Dawbarn, giving details of Elvis' early recording history and background. Also included is the interesting fact that when Elvis first appeared on American TV he drew a bigger audience than President Eisenhower drew on three TV channels, such was his popularity in the early days. Sleeve notes suggest possible earlier influences to Elvis' singing style such as rhythm and blues, gospel and hillbilly, but even more interestingly that he was strongly influenced—"despite denials by his fans"—by Johnny Ray, who was very popular at that time. That he was influenced by Johnny Ray's singing style was a widely held opinion by British Press in those days although in fact Elvis did not record a Johnny Ray number until 1960 for the "Elvis Is Back" LP and this was of course "Such A Night".

The American album (LPM 1254) had the same front cover but a different back cover which had far less comprehensive sleeve notes than British version. Notes gave some information on how he got started in his recording career but USA LP did have the added bonus of four very good small black and white photos of Elvis with guitar above sleeve notes. USA version also had five different tracks to British, and USA song titles were as follows: BLUE SUEDE SHOES: I'M COUNTING ON YOU: I GOT A WOMAN: ONE-SIDED LOVE AFFAIR: I LOVE YOU BECAUSE: JUST BECAUSE: TUTTI FRUTTI: TRYIN' TO GET TO YOU: I'M GONNA SIT RIGHT DOWN AND CRY: I'LL NEVER LET YOU GO: BLUE MOON: MONEY HONEY.

Title of LP in States was "Elvis Presley" and was issued in April 1956. Another point of interest is that the cover photo on this LP was changed for a time to that shown on American EP "Just For You" (EPA 4041). This has same

cover as British EP "Strictly Elvis" (RCX 175). Cover shows Elvis wearing a lilac-and-white striped shirt under a red jerkin and playing guitar. Current USA album has now returned to original cover photo.

The HMV LP was deleted in 1958 and it was not until 1972 that RCA decided to re-issue this LP. They chose the American version for re-release and gave it a completely new cover sleeve. New cover has photo of Elvis in colour from his NBC TV Special with title of LP "Rock 'n' Roll" in red letters at top of album and "Elvis Presley" down left-hand side in black letters. Excellent sleeve notes by Peter Aldersley—a long-standing Elvis fan—providing details of other LPs due for re-release by RCA. All of these have now been re-issued except for "A Date With Elvis" (SF 8235).

2. ROCK 'N' ROLL NO. 2—HMV (CLP 1105)

RIP IT UP: LOVE ME: WHEN MY BLUE MOON TURNS TO GOLD AGAIN: LONG TALL SALLY: FIRST IN LINE: PARALYSED: SO GLAD YOU'RE MINE: OLD SHEP: READY TEDDY: ANY PLACE IS PARADISE: HOW'S THE WORLD TREATING YOU: HOW DO YOU THINK I FEEL.

Issued in Britain in April 1957 cover shows photo of Elvis in black and white, but wearing a green shirt against a yellow background. The title of LP "Elvis Presley No. 2" is in large white letters at bottom.

Back cover has four smaller black and white photos which show Elvis on his motorcycle, reading fan mail, on horseback whilst making film "Love Me Tender", and in his swimming pool. All vintage photos these and very good. Superb sleeve notes including the information that on the "Old Shep" track Elvis played piano, the first time he had ever played on record. This LP was re-released in Britain in 1963 on RCA (SF 7528) since the original HMV LP had been deleted long before in 1958.

New front cover shows Elvis in a lilac-and-white striped, open-necked shirt with his guitar. "Elvis" in large red letters is shown in top left-hand corner whilst title of LP and song list are shown in black down right-hand side of cover. Sleeve notes on back same as before with the one exception that reference to Elvis playing piano on "Old Shep" track has been omitted

Original four photos shown on HMV album have also been removed.

USA album (LPM 1382) has similar cover to RCA re-release. Only difference to front cover is that title and song lists are not shown. Another point of interest is that some early 1960s USA albums contained a slightly different take of the "Old Shep" track. This version is no longer available.

3. THE BEST OF ELVIS—HMV (DLP 1159)

HEARTBREAK HOTEL: I DON'T CARE IF THE SUN DON'T SHINE: BLUE MOON: TUTTI FRUTTI: ALL SHOOK UP: HOUND DOG: TOO MUCH: ANY WAY YOU WANT ME: DON'T BE CRUEL: PLAYING FOR KEEPS.

Issued as 10″ LP in Britain in October 1957 and now one of Elvis' rarest LPs. This record had a mainly pink cover showing Elvis playing guitar and wearing an orange jacket over a dark-brown shirt. Very good sleeve notes on back cover and these include the interesting fact that even in those early days Elvis' popularity was worldwide, since sheet music for song "Heartbreak Hotel" was on sale in London in a dozen different languages including Swedish, Japanese, Spanish and German. This LP along with the other two HMV LPs was sadly deleted in 1958 and has never been re-released in its original form although all the song tracks were re-issued on RCA on such LPs as "Gold Records—Vol. I".

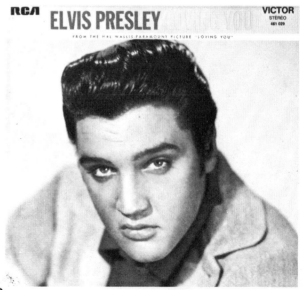

4. LOVING YOU—RCA (RC 24001)

MEAN WOMAN BLUES: TEDDY BEAR: LOVING YOU: GOT A LOT O' LOVING TO DO: LONESOME COWBOY: HOT DOG: PARTY: TRUE LOVE.

Released in 1957 on RCA as a 10″ LP to coincide with Elvis' second film the cover of this LP has a photo of Elvis (head and shoulders) wearing a grey jacket and red shirt against a blue background. He dyed his hair black for this film and cover photo shows it heavily greased in a wave. Back cover has three photos, two from film and the third a publicity photo of Elvis with two of the other stars of the film—Wendell Corey and Lizabeth Scott. Sleeve notes supply brief description of film story and details of his backing group on the LP. All tracks are from film except "True Love"—(Cole Porter number). The LP was issued as 12″ in America with same front cover. Back cover has near-similar sleeve notes but four completely different pictures from film. Side one of LP contains the seven songs from film whilst side two contains, besides "True Love", four popular ballads of the period, namely—"I Need You So", "Blueberry Hill", "Don't Leave Me Now", and "Have I Told You Lately That I Love You". The last four songs were issued in Britain in EP "Elvis Presley" (RCX 104). Another point of interest is that Elvis later re-recorded "Don't Leave Me Now" for the film "Jailhouse Rock".

The 10″ LP was deleted in the mid-sixties but all the songs were re-released on the RCA LP "Flaming Star And Summer Kisses" (RD 7723) in 1965. The additional tracks on this LP were "Flaming Star", "It's Now Or Never", "Summer Kisses, Winter Tears" and "Are You Lonesome Tonight". A point to note here is that these four songs were issued in January 1961 in the States on the EP "Elvis By Request" (LPC 128). This was also Elvis' one and only 33⅓ rpm extended play issued in the States. ("It's Now Or Never" and "Are You Lonesome Tonight" had, of course, been issued previously on singles in 1960.) Another tie-up with this EP and British LP was that the photo used on the cover of the USA EP was also used on the British LP.

Cover of British album has a 5″ × 4½″ colour photo of Elvis in top right-hand corner wearing the outfit he wore for the film "Flaming Star". To the left of this photo is "Elvis" written in large black letters whilst title of album is written in smaller lilac letters underneath. Back cover is repeat of front but only in black and white letters and without photo. This has been replaced by song title list. A point of interest about this LP is that the title track "Flaming Star" has its guitar introduction cut short, although same recording as USA version. This LP has been deleted but most of the tracks are available on the 4 LP box set Vol. 2.

5. ELVIS CHRISTMAS ALBUM (RD 27052)

SANTA CLAUS IS BACK IN TOWN: WHITE CHRISTMAS: HERE COMES SANTA CLAUS: I'LL BE HOME FOR CHRISTMAS: BLUE CHRISTMAS: SANTA BRING MY BABY BACK: O LITTLE TOWN OF BETHLEHEM: SILENT NIGHT: PEACE IN THE VALLEY: I BELIEVE: TAKE MY HAND PRECIOUS LORD: IT IS NO SECRET.

Issued in Britain in 1957 with a really outstanding cover photo of Elvis wearing a black-and-yellow zig-zag shirt, hair in large wave heavily greased shown against dark blue background. Lower right-hand corner is autographed "Best wishes, Elvis" in white letters. Back cover has photo of Elvis from film "Jailhouse Rock" plus adverts for the following records complete with photos of covers: "Loving You" LP and EPs, "Peace In The Valley" and "Elvis Presley". Back cover also contains full list of tracks on album.

On later issues of this album photo on back cover from "Jailhouse Rock", and photos of record covers were removed although adverts for records without photos remained.

This LP has long been deleted in Britain but the first eight songs listed on LP have been re-released in 1970 on "Elvis' Christmas Album" (RCA INT 1126). Other songs to be found on this record are "If Everyday Was Like Christmas" and "Mama Liked The Roses". Album also has completely new cover showing Elvis in green jacket with two vertical white stripes and with his arms folded, all against a snow-scene background. The remaining four songs—"Peace In The Valley", "I Believe", "Take My Hand Precious Lord" and "It Is No Secret" have all been re-released on RCA Camden LP "You'll Never Walk Alone" (CDM 1088) in 1971. This album also includes the following tracks "You'll Never Walk Alone", "Who Am I", "Let Us Pray", "We Call On Him", "Sing You Children" and "Swing Down Sweet Chariot". British album cover has Live Vegas Shot of Elvis wearing a cream-coloured, fringed stage outfit, whilst singing into hand-held mike.

The American versions of original British Christmas Album had same tracks but totally different covers. The first version issued in 1957 on RCA (LOC 1035) had a book version cover. Cover had a small colour photo of Elvis from film "Jailhouse Rock" (same photo as seen on "Jailhouse" EP but face only) situated near centre of album cover. This photo is surrounded by Christmas presents and decorations. Cover opened up to reveal a number of full-colour photos of Elvis (same as those seen in British LP "Gold Records—Vol. I" (RB 16069)). Also included are photos from film "Jailhouse Rock" and full details of all his available 45 rpm and 78 rpm singles. Photos of picture sleeve single covers are also shown, e.g. "Hound Dog", "Too Much" and "Love Me Tender". All in all a really outstanding cover and much sought after by collectors since being deleted.

Album was re-released in USA as LPM 1951 with completely new cover.

New cover has early photo of Elvis wearing a blue velvet shirt, looking rather sad, against a typical snow scene. This album is now deleted in USA although it is still on sale in Europe, and was replaced by new album "Elvis Christmas Album" on RCA (Camden CAS 2428). This record is the same as that issued in Britain, i.e. RCA (INT 1126) (see earlier).

6. KING CREOLE (RD 27088)

KING CREOLE: AS LONG AS I HAVE YOU: HARDHEADED WOMAN: TROUBLE: DIXIELAND ROCK: DON'T ASK ME WHY: LOVER DOLL: CRAWFISH: YOUNG DREAMS: STEADFAST, LOYAL AND TRUE: NEW ORLEANS.

Issued in 1958 as soundtrack album to film, cover has studio photo of Elvis wearing a brown jacket over white shirt and yellow scarf as dressed for film, "King Creole". Back cover has three excellent film stills including Elvis and Dolores Hart in the hotel scene, Elvis in severe pain after being stabbed in back-alley fight and in the night club just before he is asked to sing the number "Trouble". In addition are sleeve notes which supply basic story line to film.

When this LP was re-released in 1972 on SF 8231 front cover picture was retained but the three film stills photos on back cover were removed. It is interesting to note that the EP version of "Dixieland Rock" track has cut off introduction and also that the "Lover Doll" EP version is completely different to LP version, the Jordanaires being absent on EP version.

7. ELVIS GOLDEN RECORDS (RB 16069)

HOUND DOG: I LOVE YOU BECAUSE: ALL SHOOK UP: HEARTBREAK HOTEL: YOU'RE A HEARTBREAKER: LOVE ME: TOO MUCH: DON'T BE CRUEL: THAT'S WHEN YOUR HEARTACHES BEGIN: I'LL NEVER LET YOU GO: LOVE ME TENDER: I FORGOT TO REMEMBER TO FORGET: ANY WAY YOU WANT ME: I WANT YOU, I NEED YOU, I LOVE YOU.

Issued in Britain with book cover in 1958. Front cover has photo of Elvis' face set on a gold disc with a large number of other gold discs suspended behind. All are shown against red background. Cover of book opens up to reveal nine full-colour pics of Elvis plus adverts for his LPs "Loving You" and "Elvis' Christmas Album" as well as EPs "Peace In The Valley", "Elvis Presley" and "Jailhouse Rock". Photos of these record sleeve covers are shown in colour. There is also a full page of really superb sleeve notes supplying details of recording history of songs on album. Back cover has full-length photo of Elvis dressed

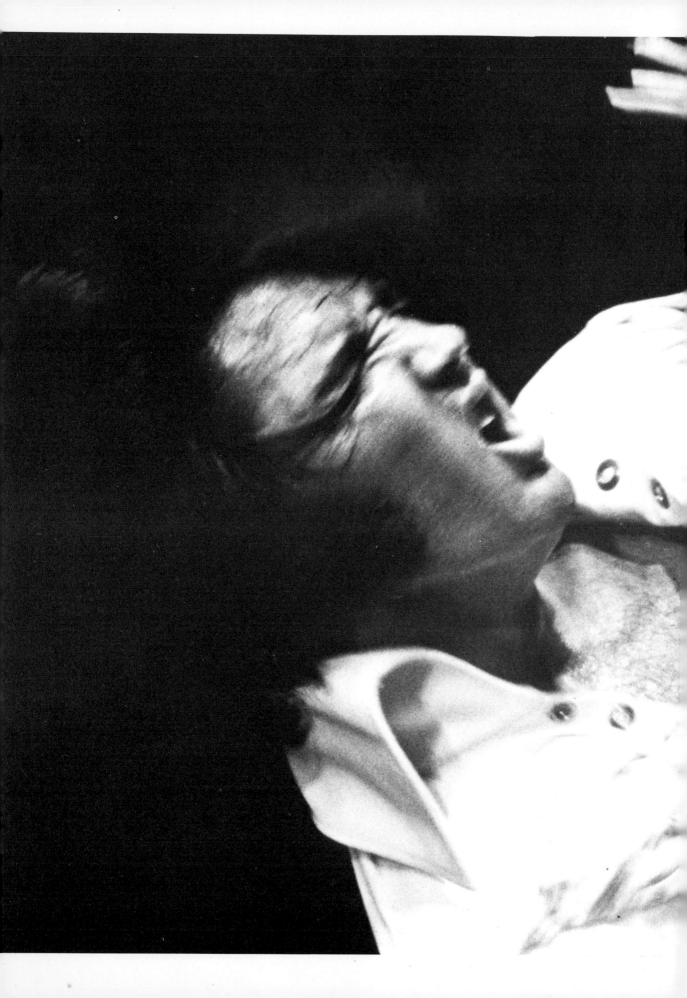

in brown trousers, red jerkin, white shoes and with a Gibson guitar slung around his shoulders, against yellow background. Title tracks are listed in top right-hand corner of back cover. There was a further issue with different cover for this LP before it was deleted. This album retained front cover but back cover now had a reduced photo of Elvis with guitar (although exactly same photo) plus three small colour photos beside it.

Inside open-out cover a complete change has occurred. Gone are the nine full-colour pics and colour photo adverts for Elvis' records. Sleeve notes remain but are resited to reverse side of front cover. Opposite these notes is a photo of Elvis' face set in a gold disc (same as shown on front cover), against a white background. This gold disc is surrounded by adverts (no photos of covers) for the LPs "Christmas Album", "King Creole", "Loving You" and EPs "Peace In The Valley", "Elvis Presley", "Jailhouse Rock" and "Elvis In Tendermood".

This album was re-released in Britain in 1970 on RCA (SF 8129) with completely different cover design. Front cover has photo of Elvis from his NBC TV Special, wearing all-leather suit and playing guitar against dark background. Back cover of album shows sleeve notes as issued on original release. All song titles as original issue.

The USA album (LPM 1707) was different to original British in that it did not have a book cover and also had four different song tracks. These were "Loving You", "Jailhouse Rock", "Teddy Bear" and "Treat Me Nice". These four numbers had been replaced on British LP by "I Love You Because", "You're A Heartbreaker", "I'll Never Let You Go" and "I Forgot To Remember To Forget". The reason for these changes in song tracks in Britain was that these tracks were unobtainable in Britain (unlike the other numbers which had previously been issued on singles) and RCA decided this was a good way to get them issued. Cover of USA album has same front cover as original British release. Back cover has same sleeve notes that are to be found inside original British album. The reason why a book cover version not issued in States was that all these same colour photos, as in British book cover had been earlier issued inside "Christmas Album" (LOC 1035). It is interesting to note that another version, with spoken words of "I Love You Because" was issued in 1973, although first recorded in 1954, on the album "A Legendary

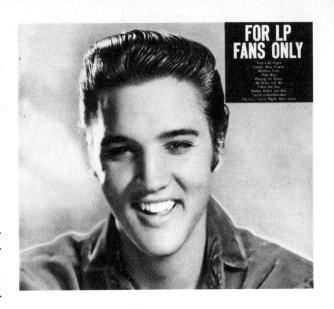

Performer, Vol. I". A different take of "I'll Never Let You Go" is available on "Good Rocking Tonight" (Bopcat album).

8. ELVIS (RD 27120)

THAT'S ALL RIGHT: LAWDY MISS CLAWDY: MYSTERY TRAIN: PLAYING FOR KEEPS: POOR BOY: MONEY HONEY: I'M COUNTING ON YOU: MY BABY LEFT ME: I WAS THE ONE: SHAKE RATTLE AND ROLL: I'M LEFT, YOU'RE RIGHT, SHE'S GONE: YOU'RE A HEARTBREAKER: TRYING TO GET YOU: BLUE SUEDE SHOES.

ISSUED IN 1959, this album contains no less than nine of the tracks issued earlier on HMV LP "Rock 'n' Roll" (CLP 1093). Cover has really outstanding colour photo of Elvis in happy smiling mood wearing red velvet shirt against blue background. Back cover has colour photo of Elvis in Army uniform. There are no sleeve notes on this LP but it has some really outstanding numbers including many of his earliest recordings. Sadly this LP was deleted a long time ago but is still available in cassette form (No. PK 11529). The USA version of this LP (No. LPM 1990) is interesting since it had only ten tracks as follows: "That's All Right", "Lawdy Miss Clawdy", "Mystery Train", "Poor Boy", "Playing For Keeps", "My Baby Left Me", "I Was The One", "Shake Rattle And Roll", "You're A Heartbreaker", "I'm Left, You're Right, She's Gone". Title of album in USA was "For LP Fans Only" and this was shown in top right-hand

corner of front cover but otherwise same as British. A slower blues version of "I'm Left, You're Right, She's Gone" is available on bootleg– "My Baby's Gone".

9. A DATE WITH ELVIS (RD 27128)

BLUE MOON OF KENTUCKY: MILK COW BLUES BOOGIE: BABY LET'S PLAY HOUSE: I DON'T CARE IF THE SUN DON'T SHINE: TUTTI FRUTTI: I'M GONNA SIT RIGHT DOWN AND CRY: I GOT A WOMAN: GOOD ROCKING TONIGHT: IS IT SO STRANGE: WE'RE GONNA MOVE: BLUE MOON: JUST BECAUSE: ONE SIDED LOVE AFFAIR: LET ME.

Released in Britain in 1959 this LP certainly filled the gap in Elvis disc releases due to his tour of Army duty. With the exception of "Is It So Strange" all of these numbers had previously been released on HMV but were of course unobtainable at time of album release. With the issue of this album all of Elvis deleted HMV recordings were once more available on RCA label. It is of interest that the "Good Rocking Tonight" (Bopcat records LP-100) contains a slower country version of "Blue Moon Of Kentucky" rather than the faster version on this LP. The Bopcat LP also has a version of "I Don't Care If The Sun Don't Shine" complete with two false starts. Another point of interest is that in the American magazine *Strictly Elvis*, issue No. 5, it was reported that Elvis had recorded a new version of "Baby, Let's Play House" and that several American DJs had been playing the new version over American radio networks.

The cover of British LP has colour photo of Elvis in Army uniform seated at the wheel of his convertible. Cover also has three smaller pictures of Elvis along bottom. Back cover has 1960 Elvis calendar with "24th March" ringed in red. This was Elvis' probable Army demob date. In fact he was discharged earlier on 5 March 1960.

This LP has long been deleted in Britain although as mentioned earlier it was given a number SF 8235 and listed for re-release back in 1972, but to date this record has not been issued which is a pity since it means a large number of Elvis' early recordings are unavailable.

The American LP (LPM 2011) had same cover but many different tracks:

BLUE MOON OF KENTUCKY: YOUNG AND BEAUTIFUL: BABY I DON'T CARE: MILK COW BLUES BOOGIE: BABY LET'S PLAY HOUSE: GOOD ROCKING TONIGHT: IS IT SO STRANGE: WE'RE GONNA MOVE: I WANT TO BE FREE: I FORGOT TO REMEMBER TO FORGET.

Once again in Britain RCA decided to alter tracks on "A Date With Elvis" album in the same way they had done on earlier LPs in order to make available to British fans many Elvis records which had been deleted when HMV records were no longer issued. This meant that only six numbers on the American LP were retained but British fans had a bonus in that the British album ended up with fourteen tracks instead of ten tracks which the American album has.

10. ELVIS' GOLDEN RECORDS, VOLUME 2 (RD 27159)

I NEED YOUR LOVE TONIGHT: DON'T: WEAR MY RING AROUND YOUR NECK: MY WISH CAME TRUE: I GOT STUNG: LOVING YOU: TEDDY BEAR: ONE NIGHT: A BIG HUNK OF LOVE: I BEG OF YOU: A FOOL SUCH AS I: DONTCHA' THINK IT'S TIME: JAILHOUSE ROCK: TREAT ME NICE.

Released in 1960 cover has fourteen photos, all same but varying in size, of Elvis in the famous gold suit against a white background. This gold suit cost $10,000 in 1957 and was designed by Liberace for Elvis after Elvis had admired a gold jacket Liberace was wearing and had asked Liberace to design a suit for him. Back cover has studio photo of Elvis wearing a white raincoat for film "King Creole" against a blue background. There are no sleeve notes and song titles are listed on front cover in top left-hand corner.

The British album has four more tracks ("Jailhouse Rock", "Treat Me Nice", "Loving You" and "Teddy Bear") than American LP (LPM 2075). The reason for this is that these songs were issued on "Gold Records, Vol. 1" (LPM 1707) in USA. Another interesting point is that the song "Dontcha' Think It's Time" is a different version to that issued on single (flip side of "Wear My Ring Around Your Neck"). The original American cover had some photos of Elvis in gold suit but background was black instead of white as on British cover. Current USA cover now has white background same as

British. American album was also titled "50,000,000 Elvis Fans Can't Be Wrong".

Album was re-released in Britain in 1970 on RCA (SF 8151) with same tracks as original but entirely new cover. Front cover has Elvis wearing red shirt and black-and-red scarf against a deep blue background. Back cover has close-up shot of Elvis in black and white, wearing the leather outfit he wore for his NBC TV Special.

11. ELVIS IS BACK—RD 27171 (SF 5060)

MAKE ME KNOW IT: FEVER: THE GIRL OF MY BEST FRIEND: I WILL BE HOME AGAIN: DIRTY DIRTY FEELING: THE THRILL OF YOUR LOVE: SOLDIER BOY: SUCH A NIGHT: IT FEELS SO RIGHT: THE GIRL NEXT DOOR: LIKE A BABY: RECONSIDER BABY.

Issued in 1960 with open-out cover this was Elvis' first LP release since being discharged from the Army. It was also his first Stereo album. Cover shows Elvis in a cream jacket against green background. Title of album "Elvis Is Back" is in large letters on right-hand side whilst song titles are listed below on yellow background. Album cover opens up to reveal fifteen $3'' \times 3''$ black-and-white snapshots of Elvis in Army uniform both on and off duty. Back cover has colour photo of Elvis in Army working clothes and cap.

This LP was re-released later without open-out cover. New album has retained same front cover photo but back cover photo has been replaced by the same fifteen black and white snapshots, now reduced to $1\frac{3}{4}'' \times 1\frac{3}{4}''$, that were inside original open-up cover. The advance sales for this album in America were not bettered until release of NBC TV Special album.

12. HIS HAND IN MIND—RD 27211 (SF 5094)

I'M GONNA WALK DEM GOLDEN STAIRS: IN MY FATHER'S HOUSE: MILKY WHITE WAY: KNOWN ONLY TO HIM: I BELIEVE IN THE MAN IN THE SKY: JOSHUA FIT THE BATTLE: JESUS KNOWS WHAT I NEED: SWING DOWN SWEET CHARIOT: MANSION OVER THE HILL TOP: IF WE EVER MEET AGAIN: WORKING ON THE BUILDING.

Elvis' very first sacred album released in 1960 originally but re-released in 1971 on SF 8207. The same cover photo of Elvis in dark suit playing piano was used for re-release album but original cover photo was framed by white border with titles whilst new album has original photo enlarged so as to cover white border. Colour of current album has greenish tinge and is not as clear as original. Back cover of current release

contains same interesting sleeve notes, all about why Elvis is interested in gospel music etc. plus advert for "Peace In The Valley" EP (black and white photo of cover). There has occurred, however, some re-arranging of the position of these notes and title of album.

13. SOMETHING FOR EVERYBODY—RD 27224 (SF 5106)

THERE'S ALWAYS ME: GIVE ME THE RIGHT: IT'S A SIN: SENTIMENTAL ME: STARTING TODAY: GENTLY, I'M COMING HOME: IN YOUR ARMS: PUT THE BLAME ON ME: JUDY: I WANT YOU WITH ME: I SLIPPED, I STUMBLED, I FELL.

First released in 1961 and subsequently re-released in 1971 with very little change in cover design. Original cover had Elvis wearing red shirt against grey background with white framing around edges of cover. Current release has made photo look more like painting by tinting red shirt to purple and grey background to blue. The white border has also been removed and there are different title headings on new album. Back cover is almost the same on both versions with two pictures from "Wild In The Country" but original cover had adverts for records (such as "A Date With Elvis" etc.) which owing to the fact that they had been deleted have been replaced on current album cover for more recent Elvis releases.

14. BLUE HAWAII—RD 27238 (SF 5115)

BLUE HAWAII: ALMOST ALWAYS TRUE: ALOHA OE: NO MORE: CAN'T HELP FALLING IN LOVE: ROCK-A-HULA BABY: MOONLIGHT SWIM: KU-I-PO: ITO EATS: SLICIN' SAND: HAWAIIAN SUNSET: BEACHBOY BLUES: ISLAND OF LOVE: HAWAIIAN WEDDING SONG.

First released in 1961 as a soundtrack album to what is probably Elvis' most profitable film ever made. Cover shows Elvis in red Hawaiian patterned shirt playing the ukelele, whilst back cover has three photos from the film. On re-release in 1970, this same cover has more or less been used but the number of the record has been changed to SF 8145.

15. ELVIS FOR EVERYONE (RD/SF 7752)

YOUR CHEATIN' HEART: WILD IN THE COUNTRY: FINDERS KEEPERS, LOSERS WEEPERS: IN MY WAY: TOMORROW NIGHT: MEMPHIS TENNESSEE: FOR THE MILLIONTH AND THE LAST TIME: FORGET ME NEVER: SOUND ADVICE: SANTA LUCIA: I MET HER TODAY: WHEN IT RAINS IT REALLY POURS.

Released in 1965, the album cover has full-length photo of Elvis from film "Tickle Me" wearing black trousers, orange cowboy shirt and playing guitar against an orange background. The title of LP "Elvis For Everyone" is written down top right-hand side in large letters. Back cover has no sleeve notes only list of song titles.

This British album differs completely from the

American issue (LSP 3450) which has a much more interesting cover. Front cover shows Elvis behind record counter dressed in blue-and-white striped shirt whilst behind him on shelves are displayed the following USA Elvis LP records: "Elvis Presley", "Elvis", Elvis' Golden Records —Vol. I", "G.I. Blues" and "Blue Hawaii".

Beside Elvis on boards are listed song tracks on album each with an accompanying small circular photo of Elvis. Back cover shows fifteen LP covers (in colour) of Elvis' worldwide 1,000,000-dollar-sale albums. It should be noted that the USA LP has the track "Summer Kisses, Winter Tears" instead of "Wild In The Country" which was issued on British LP. Reason for this change according to RCA was that "Summer Kisses, Winter Tears" had just been released on LP "Flaming Star And Summer Kisses" (RD 7723) that very same year whilst "Wild In The Country" was only available previously on a single. Unfortunately this was a bit short sighted since this LP was only issued in Mono and also has now been deleted making the "Summer Kisses" track no longer available.

"Elvis For Everyone" was re-released in 1972

on SF 8232 with completely new cover showing close-up view of Elvis with guitar against dark background. Title of LP "Elvis For Everyone" is written down right-hand side in large letters alongside Elvis' photo. Back cover shows song listing but has the added bonus of sleeve notes by Peter Aldersley supplying recording history of many of the tracks included on album. One point of interest concerning these notes, however, is that they state that whilst LP has same tracks as previous release the running order has been

changed. Well this is not true since running order is exactly as original issue.

16. HOW GREAT THOU ART (RD/SF 7867)

HOW GREAT THOU ART: IN THE GARDEN: SOMETHING BIGGER THAN YOU AND I: FARTHER ALONG: STAND BY ME: WITHOUT HIM: SO HIGH: WHERE COULD I GO BUT TO THE LORD: BY AND BY: IF THE GOOD LORD WASN'T WALKING BY MY SIDE: RUN ON: WHERE NO ONE STANDS ALONE: CRYING IN THE CHAPEL.

Elvis' second sacred album released in 1966 and containing Elvis' only sacred No. 1 hit single "Crying In The Chapel" a hit in 1965. Cover shows Elvis in blue jacket, white shirt, and dark tie (head and shoulders) with church in background. Back cover has photo of Elvis dressed in white suit standing with arms crossed in front against blue background. To the right of this picture the song titles are listed.

The album was re-released in 1971 on SF 8206. Cover photo same but slightly enlarged and with LP title also re-arranged slightly. Back cover now has black-and-white photo of Elvis (same photo as on cover of "Elvis' Golden Records—Vol. 2" (SF 8151)) plus a general re-arrangement of song titles list to that of original release.

RESUMÉ

The LPs "G.I. Blues" (SF 5078), "Gold Records—Vol. 3" (SF 7630) and "Gold Records—Vol. 4" (SF 7924) are all currently available with more or less the exact covers as original issues so I feel no further description of these is necessary.

Since the main aim of this article has been to investigate major changes of album covers and tracks consequent on their re-release I decided not to discuss any of the following LPs, all of which were issued between 1962 and 1968, since having been deleted they have not as yet been re-released in any way near their original form. However, I think they are worth listing and they are as follows:—

"Pot Luck With Elvis"   RD 27265/SF 5135
"Girls, Girls, Girls"   RD/SF 7534
"It Happened At The World's Fair"
   RD/SF 7565
"Fun In Acapulco"   RD/SF 7609
"Kissin' Cousins"   RD/SF 7645
"Roustabout"   RD/SF 7678
"Girl Happy"   RD/SF 7714
"Harem Holiday"   RD 7767/SF 7767
"Frankie And Johnny"   RD/SF 7793
"Paradise Hawaiian Style"   RD/SF 7810
"California Holiday"   RD/SF 7820
"Double Trouble"   RD/SF 7892
"Clambake"   RD/SF 7917
"Speedway"   RD/SF 7957

Finally it should be noted that whilst none of the above albums have been re-released a few of the song titles from some of these albums have been issued on some budget-priced albums.

SOLE POSSESSION OF THE KING

Elvis dear my heart and soul.
My love for you, you'll never know.
You'll never know the way I feel,
My dreams forever will stay unreal.
I look around and I can see
A thousand others just like me,
Who love and sing and preach your name.
But tell me Elvis what do we gain?
My love for you I never ponder.
But sometimes El, it makes me wonder.
It makes me wonder are you real
And if anything for us you feel?
One day you'll come if we appeal,
And then we'll see you in the real.
But I shan't dance, rejoice or sing
FOR I ALONE do want the King.

CHRISTINE GRUDZINSKA

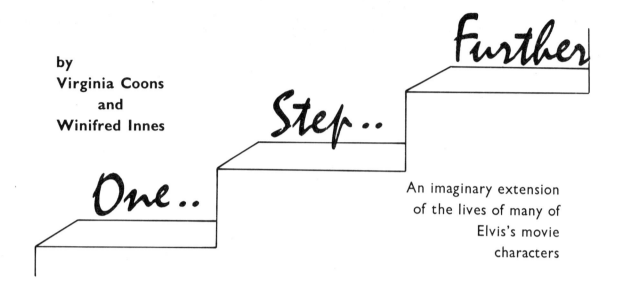

by
Virginia Coons
and
Winifred Innes

An imaginary extension of the lives of many of Elvis's movie characters

"Come on – COME ON," Elvis enthused as he edged forward in his chair, in the living room of his beautiful Palm Springs home. "Easy, Elvis," his father chuckled; as he, too, watched the televised baseball game. But his world-famous son was too engrossed in the game to pay much attention to anyone. MAN – WHAT A GAME. The score was all tied up. This was the last of the ninth; with the home-team at bat and all the bases loaded. All they needed was one good HIT. Good grief – it was nerve wracking; the suspense, as the pitcher wound up. GLOREEEE – would he ever throw the ball? Disgustedly, Elvis moaned, "What's that guy trying to do? If he doesn't stop swinging his arm round and around, like that, he's going to go straight into orbit." AH – there goes the pitch – the swing – and S-O-C-K-O, the ball zoomed clear out of the Park – A HOME RUN. "We did it – WE DID IT," Elvis shouted, happily, as he brought his right hand down against the arm of the chair. "Ooooopppsss," he muttered; for the chair-arm just sort of sagged as it split apart and dropped to the floor. Vernon Presley sighed; then chuckled as he scolded, "I suppose I ought to be used to this by now; you and that Karate bit. I'm glad this is your house, son." Much subdued; Elvis nodded – shrugged and sadly agreed, "Yeah. You know, I lose more chairs like this."

At this moment Joe, an employee, entered and gave Elvis a thick sheaf of papers. "Here's the information you wanted, El ... complete reports as to the present whereabouts of certain relatives you were once so closely associated

with. You know what puzzles me, though, why do all these guys look so much like you? Look! the investigators included pictures of most of them, and they are practically carbon copies of you. Can you explain this?" Elvis grinned and offered, "Maybe it's because we had some common ancestors – or something. How should I know?" Joe grinned and settled himself in an easy-chair as he quipped, "Ask a silly question, get a silly answer."

The much-wanted report at last in his hands, Elvis got to his feet as he said, "Excuse me. I think I'll study these out by the pool, where it's quiet." "We can turn the television off, Elvis," his father offered. But the dark-haired film star replied, "Naw; you all just go ahead and enjoy your programmes. Really, I'd kind of like to get some air, anyway."

Settled in a comfortable lounge chair, beside the inviting blue waters of the shimmering pool, Elvis crossed his grey-trousered legs and began to read.

First on the list was DEKE RIVERS; the orphaned boy who had parlayed a song and a wiggle into big-time stardom with Tex Warner's Band. Ahhhh, Deke was doing just fine, although he'd retired from show business shortly after marrying little Susie Jessup. He'd made a fortune for himself and all those associated with them. Deke and Susie owned a beautiful farm; bordering her parents' property. He was never lonely any more, never afraid, for he was surrounded by love. There was a little Deke Junior aged eight and a pretty little miss of five, who's

148

name was Glenda, in honor of the publicity woman who had given Deke the opportunity of a lifetime.

Well, good, Elvis thought, it was great to know everything was so well for Deke and Susie. He sighed, with some misgivings, though, as he wondered how in the world Deke had been able to forsake the glories of show-business. But that was Deke's privilege ... he'd simply realized where his true happiness could be found. Even after reasoning, thusly, Elvis found this difficult to accept. Why? Was it because it aroused questions within himself. Had he, himself, been wise to keep going? But he knew there was only one answer to this. He couldn't quit. He loved show-business. Had loved it right from the start. SHOW-BUSINESS — there was a kind of magic about it ... and he argued, aloud, "Stop worrying. So Deke quit, but you're not Deke. You're happy, right where you are."

He'd been so lost in thought he hadn't realized he'd spoken aloud, and he was startled when there was a step behind him and his father cautioned, "Careful, son, you know what they say about people who talk to themselves." Elvis chuckled and replied, "I'm still safe, Dad. So far, I'm not getting any answer."

As the elder man took a chair, Elvis handed him the report about Deke Rivers as he invited, "Here — read this one, while I study the next report."

Let's see; this cousin's name was Vince Everett. He'd had quite a bad time of it. Had gone to jail for manslaughter; serving fourteen months and had returned to society a very embittered soul. Then he'd met Peggy Van Alden, and gradually, as their friendship grew to love, he'd found a new life. Peggy helped him in another way too. She helped him launch his singing career and, for a while, everything had been frantically wild. There were so many personal appearances that he could barely call a minute his own. There were movies, too, and he managed to perform in a few very successful ventures. It was just about here that he decided this wasn't exactly what he wanted of life. He'd made plenty of money and could do as he pleased. Therefore, Mr. and Mrs. Everett, formerly Peggy Van Alden settled in a pleasant suburb in Connecticut. Vince's money was invested wisely, but he kept busy with his own recording company, cutting an occasional disc, every now and then, just for old time's sake and to please his many fans.

Elvis raised his eyebrow as he read this, musing aloud, "This is a foxy guy. You know, I might even end up recording for his company, some day. At that, though, I'm glad he didn't give up show-business completely." "Mmmmmm-mmmmm," Vernon Presley murmured, not quite understanding his son and lost in his own thoughts of the report he was reading.

"Never mind," Elvis smiled as he turned back to reading. Ah — nice — there was a six-year-old Vince Junior on the scene too and a baby brother of two years; little Malc. Both boys resembled their daddy.

Elvis handed this report to his dad, too, as he said, "So far, so good. I'm glad they are doing so well. You know, we're going to have to arrange a re-union." "Yeah," the elder Presley nodded.

Ah — here was the report on Mr. and Mrs. Danny Fisher. Good — he'd married the little girl he'd met while helping his unsavory acquaintances rob the store where she worked. Even from the start, Nellie had been loyal to him, for she'd known he was part of the gang, and she hadn't turned him in. But it had been a rough old road for Danny before he'd solved his problems ... and managed to free himself from the underworld boys, Max and the hoodlum crowd. In the midst of all these troubles Danny had found success; singing in the Beale Street Clubs of New Orleans. How he kept his sanity, amidst blackmail and murder, is another story, but suffice to say that he did.

Saddened at the death of Ronnie, he'd turned to Nellie for comfort. With Max no longer alive to pose any threats, Danny's return to the Clubs of Beale Street proved so successful that he was now in partnership with Charlie La Grand. Of course, Charlie was more than a business partner now; he'd married Danny's sister, Mimi, and was "family". Danny's happiness had been complete when his father had finally approved of it all and had come into the business too. Oh, yes — Papa Fisher not only approved but took over as Danny's manager.

Elvis howled with laughter as he read this. The idea of the meek, elder Mr. Fisher managing Danny was too much to believe. Danny did as he pleased; at least he always had. But wait — all troubles were over, and Danny wouldn't have to be so rough now. In fact, all along he'd yearned for his father's understanding. Now he had it!

Elvis glanced at his own wonderful father and realized what it must have meant to Danny — the reconciliation between him and his dad. Yes — this was something he could understand, all right.

Back to the report — ah — good — Maxie's hoodlum ring had been completely routed, upon their leader's death. All the Clubs on Beale Street operated honestly now — and Danny's songs were carefree and straight from the heart. Every now and then, though, someone still requests him to sing "TROUBLE", just the way he'd belted it out for Maxie — a long time ago ... and he never refuses.

Happily, Nellie would have her first baby in a

few months – and she was hoping to name the youngster Danny Junior.

Elvis sighed contentedly as he passed this report to Vernon, who smiled as he remarked, "More good news, eh? – Keep 'em comin'!"

Next on the list was Tulsa; the homesick, American soldier, stationed in Germany. Tulsa had had three ambitions:

1. To get out of the Army.
2. To marry Lily – the beautiful dancer at the Club Europe.
3. To open a night club in America, where he could perform, with two of his buddies.

Well, in due time; Tulsa's tour of duty with the Armed forces had come to an end, and it had been a happy day when he clutched his honorable discharge in his hand. Step one – realized.

The other two ambitions hadn't been that easily accomplished. Oh, Lily was deeply in love with Tulsa, all right, and wanted to marry him, but it wasn't so easy for an American soldier to get permission to marry a German girl. It had taken time to get through all the formalities, and Tulsa sometimes felt as if the War Department in Washington was making a door-to-door survey in the matter ... you know, asking the whole United States if it was all right for him to marry her.

Therefore he got his discharge papers at just about the same time he received official permission for the marriage. What do you know? It had been a double wedding; for Cooky had obtained permission to marry Lily's room-mate – the lovely Tina.

Their honeymoon? Why, the boat trip to the United States, of course. What fun it had been too, for they were all so happy. Rick and Marla; with their darling, baby son – whom Tulsa and Lily would probably always refer to affectionately as "Tiger", journeyed to America too. After all, Tulsa, Rick and Cooky were "THE THREE BLAZES" ...

A former Sergeant gave 'them some financial assistance; making it possible for the boys to open their Night Club in Oklahoma. Tulsa's unusual advertising attracted the crowds – that first night, and after listening to him sing they kept returning. In fact, so successful were the THREE BLAZES that it was necessary to book reservations to the Club now. They were booked solid.

Everyone had been happy, with the exception of Lily, who missed the excitement of the stage. Understanding this, Tulsa changed the name of his act to THE THREE BLAZES plus the DYNAMIC LILY. Now everyone was happy.

The last line read, "No children."

Elvis frowned and gave this report to his

father and sighed: "It's not right. If anyone's the father type, it's Tulsa. He ought to have six kids." Dryly, Vernon chided, "He'd make medical history, if HE did." Grinning wryly, Elvis scolded, "You know what I mean."

Vernon paused and held one hand up, indicating he wanted silence as he said, "Wait, Elvis. You missed this notation on the back of the report." With this, Vernon read aloud: "Upon speaking with Lily we were told that she is giving Tulsa a little time to get used to baby sitting with Tiger and a few others. After all, Tulsa is inclined to panic at the sight and sound of a baby's tears. Soon, though, he'd be rocking a cradle in his own home. To quote Lily: "When this time comes, I will pack my dancing costumes away for good. Raising a Tulsa Junior will be a full-time career – especially if he's like his father." Softly, she added, "I'm praying for that."

"Amen," Elvis chuckled. "She said a mouthful about it being a full time career. Man – I never knew anyone like Tulsa for getting into so many innocent scrapes."

The next page was nearly blank – except for one typewritten line;

Pacer Burton – deceased.

Somehow this saddened Elvis; even though he knew all along that Pacer was dead. Indeed,

even if he hadn't been killed by the Kiowa's, he'd be dead by now. Poor Pacer, he'd died so young and for such a lost cause. Racial Intolerance. There was still so much of it in the world today. Pacer had been such a brave soul, and Elvis wished they'd been truly related – rather than just related to Pacer's white father. Strange except for the fact that Pacer's skin was a bit darker; the Presley resemblance was very great. Hummmmmmmm.

What was Glenn Tyler doing these days? Hmmmmmm – he'd zoomed through college at the head of his class and was now studying further – in the capitals of Europe. He'd written two highly successful novels, and was wealthy enough to do as he pleased. Critics hailed him as the finest young author on the journalistic scene. He corresponded with Betty Lee; always encouraging her to date other men.

As for Nory, his wealth had given him the pleasure of helping her escape her unhappy home life. No more did she have to put up with her brutish father. She and her baby were settled in a comfortable little cottage many miles from town. In her most recent letter Nory advised him she'd met a fine young man and would soon be married ... if he, Glenn, had no objections – that is. So next time he wrote her a note he'd tell her that he, too, was planning a wedding – just as soon as he got back to the United States ... to the lovely Irene Sperry.

Yes – he still loved Irene – time had only made that more clear to him. Sure – there was a big difference in their ages – and people would talk. Well – let them. It was HIS life and IRENE'S ... and they'd both decided their LOVE was right. After all, Glenn was much older than his tender years – life had been cruel to him, and he'd had to grow up faster than most boys. On the other hand, Irene had kept youthful in spirit, by working with the very young. Both Glenn and Irene believed their marriage would be ideal.

"Another happy one," Elvis told his dad as he added the new report to those his father was already reading.

The next report read; "GATES, OF HAWAII" – and it told of the great success of the Tourist Agency owned and operated by Chad Gates and his beautiful wife ... the former Maile Duval. Chad had argued and fought against working for his own father; insisting he wanted to make his own way in the world. Then he'd solved it all by forming a sort of partnership. Yes, sir, THE GREAT SOUTHERN HAWAIIAN FRUIT CO. gave GATES, OF HAWAII, all it's tourist trade – on a percentage basis, and this, in itself, was enough to secure success.

The sign over Chad's office could well read: "GATES AND SONS, OF HAWAII", now for there were three of them – ages five, three and one; but as Chad had said to Maile in the very beginning – "GATES IS PLURAL."

Elvis turned the pages and chuckled before he read one line. Somehow, just reading the name of TOBY KWIMPER was enough for a smile or two on its own merit.

Ah – yes – he'd married pretty little Holly Jones. Good – and Elvis scanned the report quickly and said, "Good old Toby. I always knew he'd be a success. Especially since success to Toby meant just plain old day-to-day living. This kind of a guy really takes life in stride. He's got the right sense of balance for accomplishing his goals without setting the world on fire.

"They've got a little boy, Toby Junior, just barely past one year old. Says here that they are now adding onto their house in Florida because, like Grandpa Kwimper, they keep collecting every stray little waif that wanders across their path. That Toby and Holly sure have great big loving hearts, don't they, Dad?"

He didn't wait for any answer before he added; "Make a note to send Toby what he needs to finish that house and then some; okay? I'd like to help. Only remember; he won't accept charity, so make it look like he won something – fair and square, eh?" Vernon nodded – smiling proudly at the man who was the joy of his life.

Oh, here was the report on Walter Gulick, the accidental prize-fighter – Pride of Cream Valley, Kid Galahad. Poor guy, all he wanted to do was earn enough money in the prize-ring to marry Rose Grogan and buy a garage. What do you know? He'd managed to do both – and before he'd ruined his good looks too. Elvis winced; yikes, who'd written THAT? This report must have been compiled by a woman. Oh, well ...

Yes, Kid Galahad and Rose were a happy couple – proud of their home; their respectable standing in Cream Valley and, most of all, proud of their little daughter, who, incidentally, was the picture of her lovely mother.

"Nice – real nice," Elvis said. "No problems here."

Ah – now this was a guy Elvis had really worried about; Ross Carpenter. This cousin had wasted so many years on a dream. Yes – he'd worked hard to try and earn the money to buy the boat his father had built. Actually, he'd helped his father build "THE WEST WIND" – but on the very day it was completed his beloved father had died. Ross had been young – too young to realize he could have found a home with his cousins on the mainland. So he'd lived with strangers – hating the idea of charity and yearning for the day when he could stand on his own feet. Still, his dreams persisted – to OWN "THE WEST WIND". Then he'd fallen in love

*Pencil sketch by
Colin Brodie*

with Laurel Dodge, and she helped him realize that it wasn't the boat he'd wanted, after all. She made him understand that the boat was only a symbol to a grief-stricken boy — that in trying to acquire it he was only searching for his lost father . . . who was no longer alive. Yes — Ross agreed, Laurel was right . . . and so they were married.

Trouble was, Laurel was rich and spoiled, and Ross wasn't the kind of man to settle for the life of a hen-pecked husband. He wouldn't agree to live on her money, and she threw tantrums because he wouldn't join her "jet-set" crowd. Truly — they were worlds apart and both finally realized their mistake . . . that they should never have married. They parted friends and were both glad there had been no children, for in divorce it's always the young who suffer most.

Laurel decided on a world cruise after the divorce, and Ross went back to his former position — assisting rich sports-fishermen to get the big ones — marlin, etc. Ross was happy now — earning his own way and working hard to build up a fleet of fishing boats that he could call his own.

Elvis sighed — admiring Ross for his honesty. Many a man would have endured a little domestic warfare for a ticket to wealth, but Ross was a proud man. As he gave this report to his father, he said, "Mark this one special, too. I want you to send Ross a cheque to cover this fleet he wants. But whatever you do, don't let him know it's just from me. He won't accept charity of any form; he's a little more worldly than Toby, so you'll have to think of something more clever than a prize. For a moment, Elvis stared blankly at his dad, but couldn't think of anything to suggest. With a wave of his hand, he shrugged and added, "Ohhhhh — you'll think of something." The elder Presley raised an eyebrow as he echoed, "Oh sure — I'll think of something." But he chuckled, as Elvis thankfully said, "I knew I could depend on you."

Next came Mike Edwards and Diane Warren; Mike was the flyer who fell head-over-heels in love with the little nurse he'd met at the Seattle World's Fair. Yes, they'd been married. Diane gave up all ideas of joining the Space-program as she settled down as a happy wife. Mike was doing well. He'd been accepted into the Space-program and was next in line for promotion; the big one — yes, he'd be the next man selected to go into orbit. Diane was both proud and worried, but she covered it all when she told everyone who'd listen, "Mike can do anything and did you know, he's the most handsome man in the whole space-program?" Their little twin daughters, aged two and christened Ivy and Ellen, agreed with their beautiful mother — daddy was fun.

"This will please you, Dad," Elvis said as he gave his father the report. "You always did like Mike and Diane."

Oh, boy, now here was another couple he'd worried about, Mike Windgrin and Margarita Dauphine. Like Ross and Laurel, Mike and Margarita were of two different worlds. Mike was part of a circus act with his family THE FLYING WINDGRINS. Margarita was a deposed princess, who with her father had fled to Mexico. Mike, too, had fled to Mexico, but for an entirely different reason. He'd .been troubled over the accidental death of his brother; blaming himself for the aerial accident. His grief robbed him of his ability to perform; caused him to sweat with fear — so much that he couldn't even dive from the high board into a swimming pool. But in time he'd conquered his fears, realizing that his brother's death was, indeed, a tragic accident.

About to marry Margarita, Mike had second thoughts and discovered she had doubts too. Sure — they loved each other, but Margarita could never face the kind of life Mike intended to lead. Travelling, even with a big-name circus, was rough and not the security Margarita was looking for. So they'd called the marriage off . . . remaining the best of friends.

Little Raoul was still with Mike though; had journeyed to the States with Mike. It hadn't been difficult to arrange the boys' entrance into the United States. After all, Raoul was an orphan, even if he did have many cousins. The Mexican authorities agreed that Mike would do well by Raoul. So Raoul travelled all over the world with the Circus and his idol, Mike. His only complaint was that Mike insisted on many hours of schooling each day. Mike was often heard to say, "I don't know if Raoul is going to be the best darn lawyer in the country or the best con-man that ever lived."

Elvis nodded and told his dad, "I think these people made the right decision. See if you don't think so, too." "Okay," Vernon replied, "only give me time. You're a little ahead of me."

Elvis stretched, yawned and murmured, "All this reading is making me sleepy, but I've got to see this through. Oh — this one concerns our hill-billy cousins: Josh Morgan and Jody Tatum." Silently, then, he scanned the report. Josh Morgan and Azalea Tatum, Well, what do you know? They hadn't married, after all. Josh had been called back to duty in the Air Force, and while he'd been away both he and Azalea decided not to wed — each other, that is. It seems that Josh had "got used" to big city ways and couldn't face going back to mountain life. Azalea wouldn't have any part of the big city, and so that was that. But now, Jody Tatum had married the little Wac, Midge Reilly. Midge took to mountain life like she was born to it, and Jody was so happy he stopped chasing the Kitty-hawks completely.

Lucky Jackson – the racing champ. He'd married a swimming instructor in Las Vegas, Rusty Martin. They were very happy. Lucky gave up racing, and he and Rusty were the singing darlings of the Las Vegas night-club circuit. Life was a ball to them.

"Yeah," Elvis nodded in approval; "I always thought these two were Special Swingers."

Ah – yes, they had one child – a little baby boy named Tony. They had a lot of time with Tony – leaving the child with a special nurse only when they had to rehearse or give a performance. Chances were little Tony would grow up on stage.

"Good – good," Elvis beamed as he gave the page to his father.

Next? Charlie Rogers; rough, tough, devil-may-care – quick to take offence and more inclined to strike first, if he thought someone was out to get him. In a way, he was much like another cousin, Vince Everett, and just like Vince, headed for trouble. Forced to stay with a failing carnival while his motorcycle was being repaired, he'd ended up saving the show from financial collapse with his unique singing talent.

It had been a double wedding for Charlie and Cathy; the quiet daughter of the carnival manager – and Maggie and Joe. Charlie had changed, by now he no longer thought the world was against him. He'd found his place in the sun.

"Ever wondered what happened to Rusty Wells, the singer, and Valerie, Big Frank's daughter?", Elvis asked his dad. "Well, yes – now that you mention it, I have," Vernon replied. "It says that Rusty married Valerie and they're doing fine. Rusty's still singing with his combo and has a guaranteed contract, at a fantastic salary, on Big Frank's night-club circuit in the middle-west."

"Okay, okay," Vernon replied. "Read it to yourself; I'm still two cousins behind." Elvis chuckled and pursued the report further.

There was only one trouble here. Rusty flatly refused to tag along with any of Big Frank's underworld connections. Big Frank often threatens Rusty with any manner of things, but everyone knows he'd never have his son-in-law harmed. Rusty brings in the crowds, and besides, he's a good husband to Valerie. Furthermore, the kids sort of "buttered up" Grandpa Frank when they named their little boy; what else? Frank – how about that?

Elvis chuckled and exclaimed, "That Rusty, leave it to him. He knows all the angles. I wasn't

too worried about him."

Next came Lonnie Beale and Pam Merritt. Lonnie had met Pam when he'd taken a job at a health ranch; between Rodeo engagements. Pam was an instructor, but headed for danger because she was the sole possessor of a treasure map. Actually, the treasure was rightfully hers, as it had belonged to her grandfather, but many others thought differently. Lonnie had helped her find the gold — had saved her from her tormentors and fallen in love with her at the same time.

They were married and Pam used the money to build their very own ranch. However, she was very wise. She knew Lonnie would never settle down to quiet life — away from his beloved rodeos. Besides, he loved to sing for people too. Therefore, she built a special kind of ranch suited to keep Lonnie busy and "right at home" ... a Dude Ranch. Lonnie loved people, and everybody loved him; he organized riding parties; rodeos and sang to his heart's content at various outings. Yes, it was fun for everybody.

Pam was happiest that she'd been able to separate Lonnie from his Rodeo riding. Oh, how she shivered to think he might get hurt. The rodeos he arranged here on the Dude Ranch were strictly "dude". Her man was safe. However, of late, she had another worry. Lonnie kept talking about teaching their son to ride a horse before he could walk. My goodness, the baby wasn't even born yet, and what if it wasn't a boy, but a sweet little girl? Oh, well, so she'd probably ride too. Pam idolized Lonnie — loved him more than life. He was her whole world and everything he wanted was all right with her. "Nice," Elvis said, turning this report over to his father.

Ah, now here was a match that was something else. Johnny Tyrone, the American film star, and Princess Shalimar of the Middle East. Their worlds were so very different. But evidently this was a case of true love, for after a brief return to the United States Johnny had sold all properties and cancelled all commitments to take his homesick bride back to her own world. "I'll never leave you," he'd told her, "and if this is where you want to be then I'll stay here too."

They lived happily at her summer palace, and Johnny invested his wealth wisely in the country's main asset — OIL. And so — at a very early age Johnny Tyrone retired. If it could be called retirement — since his average day would surely tire the heartiest soul. He was a rugged individual, and right now was learning many new Middle East sports.

As for the Princess, she was extremely happy. For one thing, she knew she would always be her husband's ONLY wife. Unlike her people, he didn't believe in polygamy. In fact, he hadn't, nor would he give up his western beliefs. Strangely enough, her people accepted him, for he was man enough for them to admire. Yes — the Princess had every reason to be very proud and happy.

Oh — here was the memo he'd asked to see about Frankie and Johnny. They'd lived in a bygone era, but nonetheless, Johnny was kin and he'd asked the investigators to find out what had happened after he'd married Frankie.

When Frankie thought she'd fatally shot Johnny, she'd promised him anything — if he'd only live. In fact, she'd said, "Oh, Johnny, I love you; you can gamble all you want. I want you, any way you are." And the rascal had lived. But wait — it seems that after he was married he'd lost all interest in gambling. Ha — he complained that Frankie had taken all the fun out of it when she quit nagging him about it. Now that it was no longer forbidden it wasn't any fun. What a nut!

Anyway — they didn't go to Broadway as they'd intended, but saved their money and bought their own show-boat. They'd had a ball running it — singing and dancing the entire length and breadth of the great Mississippi river. They'd lived long, happy lives and raised a lovely family of six — three girls and three boys.

Rick Richards — still in the tourist business in Hawaii; in partnership with Danny. Many people expect him to marry his secretary; affectionately referred to as Friday — but so far no date has been set. Since Rick dates no other girls but Friday, the wedding can't be far off — truly — another "wolf" has bit the dust.

Mike McCoy — another cousin, still single and loving the life of a carefree, touring entertainer. Sometimes he stops singing long enough to win the Cup at another race. A winner for sure in whatever he tries. "Yea," Elvis cheered. "Keep spinning Mike — never SPINOUT."

Ted Jackson — another bachelor. At first it was thought he'd marry Jo Symington, but although they have remained good friends, they decided against marriage. For one thing, Ted never did master Yoga, and it was wearisome talking to a girl while she stood on her head for hours at a time. Not only that — it put an awful kink in his neck. For a singer — this was murder. And that's what Ted was doing these days — singing at his friend's little club, on the water front.

Guy Lambert and Jillian Conway, these two were Mr. and Mrs. now and were touring Europe together. It wasn't exactly all pleasure, for Guy had to finish his singing commitments with Georgie and the G. Men. Guy didn't mind

– in fact, singing was a pleasure for him and, actually, Jill didn't mind either – for she delighted in the knowledge that this entertainer, who had all the ladies in the audience sighing, was her very own husband.

As for the difference in their ages – Guy found Jill quite mature for her age and wonderful to be with – and my gosh, she wasn't so all-fired old. Yes – life looked rosy for these two.

No sooner had Elvis finished reading this last line, when he felt rough hands on his shoulder – shaking him, and a familiar voice called, "Elvis – Elvis – come on, son, wake up. It's time for that baseball game you wanted to see."

With a start, Elvis sat up straight. My gosh – he'd fallen asleep in his chair in the living room – while waiting for the game. He sighed and stretched – then grinned as he told his dad, "I just had the most unusual dream. Remember how I've always told you how deeply involved I get with each "character" I portray on screen?

"While I'm doing that role; I really put myself in that character's place. For a fact; I became Mike McCoy – or Ted Jackson – or any of the others. Well – I've always wondered what really happened to these people when the last scene faded away. Did they all live happily ever after – or what? Now I know – my dreams just solved it all – for a while – until other 'last scenes' fade away, that is."

Vernon Presley smiled proudly and soothed, "Well – don't worry, son. I'm sure you'll have another dream and solve it all."

"Game's on," Joe advised. To which Elvis remarked, "I've already seen it. It was in the dream, too." Of course, he was howled down, and he grinned as he slid to the floor and curled up close to the television. "I'll watch from here," he explained. "It'll be easier on the furniture if the game plays out like it did in my dreams."

Everyone laughed at him – it would be difficult not to – since Elvis had a way of saying things that made them funnier than they really were.

Elvis frowned, though, as he said, "I dreamed of everyone but poor old Clint Reno." "Well, of course," Vernon told him, "You knew Clint got killed. He was shot – remember?" "Yeah," Elvis drawled. "But Pacer was there – and so was Frankie and Johnny – and by now they'd naturally be dead anyway."

"Don't worry about it," Vernon soothed. "Dreams are odd – so you forgot one guy – nobody's perfect." "I know," Elvis scowled. "But I thought a lot of old Clint – the poor kid really got hoodwinked – all the way around. I think I'll go back to sleep after the game and see if I can dream up a happier ending for Clint – you know, have him recover – instead of die of that wound. How'd that be?" "Suit yourself," Vernon replied. "But let's watch the game."

But it was just like his dream – play by play – and like seeing a movie for the second time. Hummmmmmmm – this was a good time to take bets on a game – might as well get some action going around here. Hummmmmmmmm – maybe he'd assumed too much of the gambling character of Frankie's rascal husband, at that. What a thought...

The ELVIS PRESLEY story

This fascinating account was written shortly before the death of The King, by the Secretary of his British fan club, Todd Slaughter.

Elvis Aaron Presley, the surviving member of twins born after a difficult birth to mother Gladys and father Vernon, entered this world on 8 January 1935. Elvis was born into a world of poverty. His home town of Tupelo in the State of Mississippi supported a segregated black and white community system, and whilst the Presley family were caucasian, their social and financial standing was that of the suppressed black community. They lived in a wooden shed!

It was the struggling ambition of Vernon Presley which took the family from the cotton-picking community of Northern Mississippi into the industrial state of Tennessee and the city of Memphis. It was 1948. Presley Snr. was working as a packer, and Presley Jnr. still at school. He had started his first year at L.C. Humes High School, but the move wasn't easy for the family. Their home accommodation was a bed-sit in a slum, and Elvis' father was working all hours to try to improve his standard of living. As for Elvis, he was continually teased and tormented in the classroom for his hick-attitudes and life styles. It could have been this continued badgering which produced Elvis Presley – the extrovert. By now Elvis had seen the gaily coloured apparel worn by

the country stars of the South East, and the purveyors of this pink paraphernalia attracted his undivided attention.

Whilst he was in Tupelo, Elvis received his first guitar. It was a present from his dad in lieu of the bicycle he really wanted, but because of his prize-winning attempt at singing "Old Shep" at the Mississippi–Alabama State Fair, more of an investment for the future. The investment was beginning to pay off. By now Elvis could play to perfection, and was star attraction at all his school festival functions. Times were still hard. To earn the honest-buck, Elvis ushered at the local movie theatre after school, and yearned for the day he could be self-supporting.

June 1953 came quickly enough. He passed his final school examinations and went into industry. His best love (at the time) was the life of the long-distance lorry driver. Elvis didn't quite make it, but left to become delivery driver for a local electrical goods company.

Several times each week, Elvis would drive past the offices of a privately owned recording studio. "Memphis Recording Services" was a subsidiary of the "Sun Record Company", both of which were operated by the legendary Sam

Phillips. One day in April, 1953, as a present for his mum, Elvis booked time to record two songs, "My Happiness" and "That's When Your Heart-aches Begin". One year later he cut another acetate of the ballads "Casual Love" and "I'll Never Stand In Your Way". This time it was studio owner Sam Phillips who operated the controls and he was so impressed with the blues quality of Presley's voice that this time he wasn't going to let him go. When he found songs he thought suitable for the Presley repertoire, Elvis was invited to make a commercial recording. The result was poor, but Phillips' interest in this young singer was high. He introduced Elvis to guitarist Scotty Moore and bass player, the late Bill Black. The chemistry worked.

"That's All Right Mama" became Presley's first commercially-pressed single on the Sun label, manufactured incidentally in both 78 and 45 rpm, and issued during August of 1954. An engineered first radio play (Sam Phillips was his own company's record plugger) on DJ Dewey Phillips' WHBQ show "Red Hot and Blue" brought in hundreds of telephone enquiries and thousands of orders. Elvis' first disc sold its way into his home town's hit parade. But the United States being a big country, Elvis' success was still only on a localised basis. The best was still to come.

Whilst the mass media in the United States during the mid-fifties was beginning to become as effervescent as European radio and TV today, the sheer size of the country was prohibitive to a small independent company such as Sun Records of Memphis. It really didn't matter too much for Elvis and his band, and although he may not have been heard of in New York, in the Southern States Elvis was becoming big box-office.

During Elvis' stay with Sun he is reported to have recorded a total of 30 or so further songs, though less than half of this number have been commercially released. The existence of the remainder is in doubt, but over the years there have been continued reports of pending illicit albums containing such tracks as "Tennessee Saturday Night", "Oakie Boogie" and "Uncle Penn". As the bridge of time widens, hopes of the "collector" must be failing, because it is virtually certain that had these tracks survived the test of time, they would have been resurrected on one of the many Presley "bootleg" albums.

The kind of music Elvis was singing in the mid-fifties had still to be tagged as "Rock 'n' Roll". In the area it was called "Rockabilly", but as Elvis pursued his recording career, and improved his stage presentation, the Presley style, as is often caricatured today, was beginning to emerge. His raw, often rude rebel-rousing performance was to evoke both negative and very positive responses from his audience, and as was to be proven in the months to follow, his bodily gesticulations, though

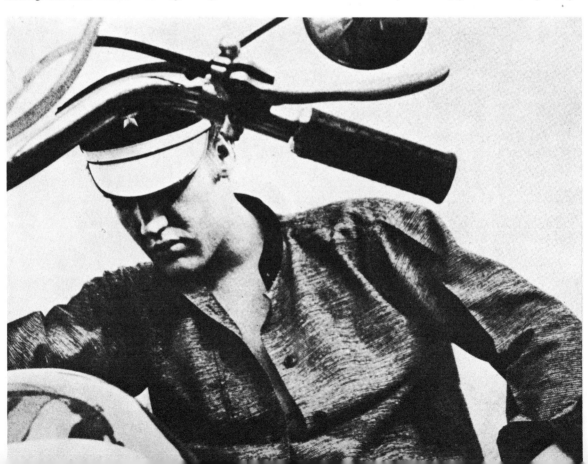

tame today, were often thought obscene.

Tennessee was the home of "country" music. To promote his talents to a wider audience Elvis had to turn towards television. In Nashville, the top programme was WSM TV's "The Grand Old Opry" (Opry being a derivation of the word Opera), yet Elvis' appearance was a disaster. However, when he was heard on Shreveport's "Louisiana Hayride" the response won him a weekly contract. With a new member added to the team, drummer D. J. Fontana, and the entertainment game now a full-time occupation, Presley was being noticed. Colonel Parker, already a millionaire from promoting and managing the country and western product, met Elvis when he was bottom of the bill of a package which starred a Parker protege. In July 1955 Elvis' fourth single for Sun, "Baby Let's Play House" climbed to Number 2 in the National chart, and Presley mania was about to be unleashed. "Mystery Train" was Elvis' fifth and final release, and the Colonel, now in command, contrived the transfer of contracts, collateral and tape masters to RCA Victor Records.

On 10 January 1956, two days following Elvis Presley's 21st birthday, he recorded his first session for RCA. Five songs were recorded at the company's Nashville studio, and the line-up of musicians included Elvis himself on guitar, Scotty Moore (lead guitar), Chet Atkins (guitar), Bill Black (bass), D. J. Fontana (drums), Floyd Cramer (piano) with vocals from Gordon Stoker and Ben and Brock Speer – three members from the Missouri-based choir known as the Jordanaires. The tracks, in order of recording, were understood to be "I Got A Woman", "Heartbreak Hotel", "Money Honey", "I'm Counting On You", and "I Was The One".

Seventeen days later Elvis was a guest on the "Tommy and Jimmy Dorsey Show" transmitted from New York on 28 January 1956. The repercussions experienced by the TV contractor concerned lasted for weeks.

For five days commencing 30 January Elvis recorded a further eight songs at RCA's New York studios, and these tracks, plus those previously in the can from the Nashville session, formed the basic ingredients of Elvis' first album LSP 1254. By April both single and album were topping the American hit parade!

Despite an abortive Las Vegas appearance,

Elvis became in "media" terms an overnight success, and record sales were echoed throughout the world. Elvis was now appearing on huge coast-to-coast US television programmes with all-time record-breaking audiences. Hosts such as Milton Berle and the late Ed Sullivan all wooed Elvis Presley into guest appearances, and it was during his second Ed Sullivan programme that he introduced America to the title song of his first movie – "Love Me Tender" – Elvis' sixteenth single release in ten months!!!

As far as the rest of the world was concerned, Elvis fans could only judge the Presley image through press and radio reports, and on disc. One thing which was for certain was the fact that our "overnight success" had arrived! Even in these early times promoters were bidding for overseas tours for Elvis Presley, but it was the Colonel's philosophy that the outside world would see Presley on the cinema screen, and on the cinema screen only!

Producer and starmaker Hal B. Wallis from Paramount Pictures had been the first producer to sign the pop giant to a seven-year contract, but "Love Me Tender", Elvis' first movie, was scooped by 20th Century-Fox. Wallis followed 20th Century-Fox's lead with "Loving You", a musical rock 'n' roller roughly autobiographical on Presley himself, and MGM's Pandro S. Berman followed smartly with "Jailhouse Rock".

On 20 December 1957 Elvis was summoned for draft into the US forces on 20 January 1958, but a letter from Elvis had the conscription delayed for 60 days – time enough to complete his fourth movie. It was "King Creole", again for Hal B. Wallis, and a film in which Elvis the Pelvis showed a natural acting talent to a doubting public.

On 24 March 1958, at the unearthly hour of 6.30 am, Elvis Presley reported to the Memphis recruitment office. Twelve hours later he was Private Elvis Presley US GI 53310761, and on his way to Fort Chaffee, Arkansas. During his enlistment Colonel Parker was busy entertaining reporters and crowds of tearful well wishers with promotional gimmicks for "King Creole".

The burning question in every fan's heart if not on their lips was of course, "Could his popularity endure a two-year enforced separation from his audience?"

So Elvis Presley became a real-life soldier. The world's press looked on to see just what was happening to the King of Rock 'n' Roll, and no US GI received more attention than Private Presley. The training camp in Arkansas was besieged daily by photograph and story-hungry reporters. The Army looked on, anxious not to give the wrong impression, but equally conscious of their responsibility and their position. Elvis too was concerned that he should receive equal treatment to his fellow soldiers. Colonel Parker assumed supreme command, and on occasions "pulled rank" over other officers.

When Elvis was transferred to his tank battalion in Texas he arrived to find that the Press and the Colonel were once again waiting to greet him. Again the Army was tolerant, and for a couple of days allowed the press more freedom than ever before inside Fort Hood, home of A Company, Second Medium Tank Battalion – Second Armored Division US Army.

It was soon time for the soldiering to start. The press had left, but again the problems for the Army were of gigantic proportions. Teenage girls, hoards of them, swarmed over the post each weekend in the hope of catching just a glimpse of the pop giant. Elvis hid. Mail arrived in lorry loads, and the 'phone never stopped ringing. It was reported that girls would impersonate Army Officers to get inside camp when they knew that Private Presley was on duty.

Suspicious of their glitter-clad colleague, soldiers gave him the cold shoulder, or tried to get at him with provocative comments. "By the left, quick – wiggle!" Others looked on, but all agreed that Elvis Presley was a regular guy.

In the early stages of Elvis' army career, Colonel Parker considered Elvis' position as a kind of moral-entertainer in the force's Special Services Dept. Many big names had been entertaining the troops in Korea, and of course it was one way to receive "special treatment" whilst at the same time working for one's country. Elvis refused, and Colonel Parker agreed. Our hero was gradually becoming the "all-American Boy".

Parents were impressed, and fans proud! Elvis was in a strong position, as the nation began to enjoy the records and movies still in the can. "King Creole" had just been released to rave reviews. Elvis had never appeared so happy. Critics for the first time were writing constructive comments, and many liked his acting talents.

On 14 August 1958 Elvis' mother died. The pop world mourned alongside Elvis. A couple of days earlier he had been given compassionate leave to join his father at his dying mother's bedside. "Oh God, everything I ever had has been taken from me!"

Ten days later Elvis was back on camp, and readying himself for transfer to Germany. Elvis had told the Press that his father and grandmother would be coming with him – it had been his mum's dying wish, and there was nothing in Army regulations to prevent this move. Any soldier when not on duty was allowed to live off camp if dependants lived within reasonably close proximity.

On 1 September Elvis and his unit began their journey to Brooklyn. The Press and the Army top brass waited. Elvis was to sail to Germany aboard the troopship *SS General Randal*. Colonel Parker was already there when Elvis and his army buddies arrived. So too was RCA. The recording company giant was there to record the highlights of Elvis' press conference. It was later to be pressed as an EP record, and achieved a million-plus sales.

When Elvis arrived in Bremerhaven the quay was packed with screaming German Elvis fans, though he managed to avoid the mass by boarding a troop train near to the vessel's unloading area. He was quickly on his way to his new base located just outside of a small town – Friedberg, which was not far from Frankfurt. Again there was a Press reception and photo session which lasted several days.

Elvis' father had found a middle-class home with four bedrooms at Goethestrasse 14, and here the family was to reside for the next eighteen months. There was still sufficient material to propagate the Presley legend in his absence, and the Colonel was continually releasing press statements as to the direction Elvis' career would take after army

service.

It wasn't until July 1959 that RCA found there was little left, except to re-issue or repackage previous releases. During the first week in August the album "A Date With Elvis" was issued. Although the material consisted of previously pressed Sun and movie soundtracks, it was good, and sold its way to the top of the US album charts. The album sleeve showed Elvis' Army discharge date encircled on a 1960 calendar.

At the same time it was announced that Elvis Presley's first post-army movie was to be a story about a US Army tank sergeant stationed in Germany. "G.I. Blues" was conceived and producer Hal B. Wallis moved a Paramount film crew to Germany whilst Presley was still in the force to shoot background material.

During his Army career both Presley Jnr. and Snr. met their prospective future wives. For Elvis it was a pretty little Air Force captain's daughter – Miss Priscilla Beaulieu, and for Vernon Presley, Mrs. Dee Elliott, a woman then married to an Army sergeant.

Finally Elvis' demob was scheduled following a couple of hoax rumours that it might be accelerated. The day before he left Germany a press conference was staged, and Elvis was asked how Army life had affected his rock 'n' roll career. "Whaal, I was in tanks, you know, and they rock 'n' roll quite a bit!"

Priscilla went with Elvis to Frankfurt air base to kiss her man goodbye, and when he arrived at McGuire Air Force Base in New Jersey during the following press reception, Nancy Sinatra was on hand to give Elvis a welcome home kiss. On 5 March 1960 Elvis Presley was a civilian.

The Colonel had not been hibernating. Recording sessions were planned, and a guest coast-to-coast welcome home TV show appearance on the Frank Sinatra programme heralded the return of the Pelvic distorter. Now it was time to go back

to the film studio!

Even Elvis Presley had to agree at a press conference that his movie appearances of the mid to late-sixties were not ideal vehicles to exercise his talents. But in all Elvis appeared in 31 films and two cinema documentaries. All 33 made money, and many broke all-time box office records.

In his early career development prior to Army service Elvis appeared in four films, and it is these movies which most Elvis Presley fans hold in highest esteem. The first, a western for 20th Century-Fox, "Love Me Tender", opened to near riot scenes in New York. "Loving You" and "King Creole" made by Hal Wallis for Paramount showed that Elvis' acting talents were beginning to develop. Between these two features "Jailhouse Rock" was unleashed onto the box office public in October of 1957. It received mixed reviews, but became very popular with cinema audiences, especially when re-released during Elvis' absence.

Six months after Elvis returned from Germany "G.I. Blues" came onto the American movie circuit. It contained a generous selection of songs, all of which were released simultaneously on an album. This was the pattern for the future. Elvis would make two or three movies each year, there would be three film albums, and perhaps one studio session from which a non-movie LP and a couple of singles would emerge. Other singles would be lifted from film sound-track albums. The formula was just right, and it worked! "Wooden Heart" from "G.I. Blues" soundtrack, whilst never issued in the USA as a single until Christmas 1964, was a number one record throughout Europe in 1961. The abundance of recorded material from both film soundtracks and studio sessions gave RCA an enormous repertoire and a greater amount of flexibility regarding worldwide releases for Elvis.

Another western, "Flaming Star", filmed in the San Fernando valley area of Los Angeles, was released at Thanksgiving in the USA, and three months later in Europe during the early part of 1961. It was Colonel Parker's plan that as often as possible Elvis' movie releases would coincide with US holiday periods. Not only would the box office be excessive during evening performances, but very very healthy from matinee showings!

"Wild In The Country" followed. It was basically a non-singing role with a semi-serious story line. Elvis fans who had been with the "King of Rock" from the early fifties found it hard to swallow. No matter, it still grossed the odd million for its makers, 20th Century-Fox, and for Elvis and the Colonel. "Blue Hawaii" is possibly Elvis Presley's best-known film, and certainly his most popular. Again it was part of the Hal B. Wallis contract for Paramount, and like all movie soundtracks, it was recorded in Hollywood, and later handed over to the record company for release. "Follow That Dream", Elvis' ninth movie, had its movie score cut at RCA's Nashville Studios during July of 1961, and the movie was subsequently released in the US over the Easter holiday period of 1962. "Follow That Dream", an amusing Hill Billy comedy, and "Kid Galahad", with Elvis taking the role of a white Muhammad Ali (yes, you too have noticed the facial similarity) were two films made by the Mirish Company (United Artists), the latter being on circuit during the summer of the same year.

Back to Paramount for "Girls, Girls, Girls", a Christmas release in the States and from the album, a worldwide single hit with the track "Return To Sender". All of Elvis' films produced hit singles, and surprisingly much of the material was commercial.

By now, and Elvis was the first to agree, he was beginning to get into a rut. His last public appearance was a charity concert in Hawaii in 1961. (This was a benefit to raise money for the USS Arizona Memorial Fund – a battleship which was sunk by Japanese dive bombers in the Pearl Harbor raids almost 20 years earlier.) He was beginning to lose contact with his audience.

The films flowed! "It Happened At The World's Fair" (MGM) April 1963; "Fun In Acapulco" (Paramount) November 1963; "Kissin' Cousins" (MGM) March 1964; and two months later the release of "Viva Las Vegas". In "Viva Las Vegas" (retitled "Love In Las Vegas" in the UK) Elvis (Lucky Jackson) portrays a would-be world racing champion after leading lady Ann-Margret (swimming instructress Rusty Martin). In all of Elvis Presley's features there was always a bevy of beauties and lots of cute kids. Family films, and at the time family entertainment. How out of context they appear, and dated, when screened on television ten years after. The mid-sixties movie makers were in general producing films far away from real-life situations, and not only Elvis was affected.

"Roustabout" (Paramount) November 1964; "Girl Happy" (MGM) January 1965; "Tickle Me" (Allied Artists) September 1965; "Harem Scarum" (MGM – retitled "Harem Holiday" for UK distribution) October 1965; "Frankie And Johnnie" (United Artists) March 1966; "Paradise Hawaiian Style" (Paramount) June 1966; and "Spinout" (MGM – "California Holiday" in the UK) October 1966. The latter was produced by Joe Pasternak, father of former BBC DJ Emperor Rosko. Elvis chasing girls, Elvis working in a carnival, Elvis after a missing millionairess, the mix was always the same. Driving fast cars, chasing fast women, and always stopping to fight the foe and sing a serenade.

In secrecy Elvis Presley married his Army sweetheart Miss Priscilla Beaulieu in Las Vegas on 1 May 1967. Presley paid 15 dollars for the licence from Clark County Court House, and the ceremony was followed by a reception and press conference at the Aladdin Hotel on the Vegas Strip. Unhappily the union ended in divorce though the couple remained friendly and jointly saw to the welfare of their only child, Lisa Marie Presley, who was born on 1 February the following year.

By 1967 cinema numbers for the Presley epic were beginning to dwindle. "Easy Come, Easy Go" for Paramount, "Double Trouble" for MGM and United Artists' "Clambake" did little to encourage fans to pass past the box office. In 1968 Elvis made his first TV appearance in seven years. In a special produced by NBC Elvis' visual image was beginning to change, and whilst the programme highlighted a cavalcade of past oldies, it was a very important step as it marked the return of Elvis to the live audience markets . . . albeit an audience specially invited for the telerecording.

The Colonel had agreed that it was time for Elvis to return to the television screen, but only for a one-off appearance. The Singer Sewing Machine Company sponsored the show and the telerecordings were executed on 27, 29 and 30 June 1968. It was Elvis' first live performance in seven years, and the artiste virtually had to be carried back to his dressing rooms at the end of the sessions. Although the audience was "invited" and only a small one at that, Elvis was reported to be highly nervous, both of appearing before people again, and of the outcome. How wrong he was. His performance was excellent, and when the show was transmitted to America on 3 December the same year, the response to Elvis live again was overwhelming! Elvis too had gotten the taste for working with an audience again.

But there were more films to follow. Three in 1968 – "Stay Away Joe" (MGM), "Speedway" (co-starring Nancy Sinatra and released in May by MGM), and "Live A Little, Love A Little" again MGM. "Live A Little . . ." has never been released in Great Britain, although it proved a popular movie in both the US and many European countries. "Charro", a fine western made for the National General Corporation was released in March 1969, and "The Trouble With Girls" (MGM) had its first run in the US two months later. A much-edited version finally made the British circuit some time later as one of the last "B" pictures. "Change Of Habit" for NBC – Universal was the last acting role for Elvis Presley. Released in 1969 in the States it was only to be shown on television for most of the rest of the world. Rightly so too. It was well acted by both Presley and co-star Mary Tyler Moore, and was typical "Wednesday Movie" material.

A new thirty-storey hotel was being constructed in Las Vegas. It was to be the resort's largest with over one thousand five hundred rooms, and the world's biggest casino. The cabaret showroom, seating two-thousand diners, was constructed behind the casino. It was to be called the International, and Barbra Streisand was scheduled to open the Showroom Internationale on 2 June. It was the ideal place for Presley to make his public return, and a deal with Bob Miller, the hotel's impresario, was concluded.

The Jordanaires, who had been backing Elvis successfully through his early live appearances and subsequently throughout his recording career, were big stars on the country circuit in their own right. They were unable to give him vocal backing in Las Vegas due to prior commitments, and group leader Gordon Stoker called this the biggest disappointment in his life. Colonel Parker's second-in-command, Tom Diskin, was busily arranging a band, whilst Elvis shopped around for his own vocalists. The Imperials, a quartet of male voices which had backed him on the "California Holiday" LP, and Atlantic Records' Sweet Inspirations, a black girl quartet, were chosen. Diskin had spoken with top session musician James Burton about the possibility of putting a group together, but he had no idea it was for Elvis until the star called him from his Memphis home to explain exactly what he wanted. The band came together – James Burton (lead guitar), John Wilkinson (guitar), Jerry Scheff (bass), and Ronnie Tutt (drums), with Larry Muhoberac (piano) and long-time friend Charlie Hodge (guitars and vocals). Female vocal support came from the Sweet Inspirations and solo vocalist Millie Kirkham. The Imperials provided the masculine harmonies.

The Elvis Presley Show followed the Barbra Streisand opening season, and Elvis was on stage twice nightly for a month. Four days of this first Las Vegas season were recorded by RCA Victor and later issued on an album. More seasons followed, and Elvis had begun to tour the States again. Elvis' third Las Vegas gig was filmed by MGM to be later distributed as "Elvis That's The Way It Is".

It was a hit throughout the world. Although no overseas tours for Elvis were ever considered by the Presley management, the outside world was at last able to see him performing live, if only on the big screen. The competence of Elvis and his fellow musicians was appreciated by all, especially his critics.

Another live-appearance film followed, and although not as successful as "That's The Way It Is", it did examine the Elvis Presley Show from other angles. The former concentrated upon Elvis' fan following and his Las Vegas cabaret. "On Tour" followed the roadshow around the States, and looked in depth at the problems created by security, transportation and presentation. A split screen technique was used continually throughout the show to give an even more convincing view as to the size of Elvis' continued following and popularity.

In January 1973 Elvis performed a 90-minute telecast which was transmitted to a world audience (at least to those countries whose TV services could afford the programme) via communications satellites. The show was beamed from the H.I.C. Arena, Honolulu, Hawaii, on 15 January.

For most of the seventies Elvis' management concentrated on live appearances throughout the United States, and two regular summer and winter seasons at the Las Vegas Hilton (formerly the International Hotel).

Todd Slaughter ended his account here, little knowing the tragic sequel which the story was to have. His words stand now as a fine tribute to a great star.

THE M.G.M. STORY

BY TERRY MAILEY JNR.

Metro-Goldwyn-Mayer was formed in 1924 and quickly became one of the most powerful film studios in Hollywood. A film with the M.G.M. trademark of Leo the Lion on it meant a film of great quality and also a film that the whole family could enjoy, for Sam Goldwyn, the studio head, insisted that the company produce films suitable for mass consumption. The studio output therefore consisted of mainly lightweight comedies and frothy musicals, with the occasional biblical epic thrown in.

Unknown actors and actresses were signed by the studio and groomed for stardom and the role-call of stars through the years is really quite impressive: Katherine Hepburn, Mickey Rooney, Judy Garland, Cary Grant, Fred Astaire, Gene Kelly, Robert Taylor, Vivien Leigh, and perhaps the biggest of them all, the legendary Clark Gable.

During the 1950s when the TV medium was taking the cinema audiences away from the theatres and keeping them at home by the TV sets, MGM began to change their policy on the type of films that they would make. Stark dramas like *Blackboard Jungle* and social commentaries like *Red Badge of Courage* were issued, in a bid to win back the vast audiences that MGM had enjoyed in their glorious past. In a bid to get out of the red MGM signed a young Rock'n'Roll singer to appear in a melodramatic role for them. His name–Elvis Presley.

Elvis was welcomed with open arms into the MGM Studios in Culver City and given the dressing room previously occupied by Clark Gable, and somehow it seemed only fitting that the King of Rock'n'Roll should be given the dressing room of the King of Hollywood. The film *Jailhouse Rock* that Elvis was signed to make for MGM was to become one of his greatest triumphs and something of a cult movie in the years to come. Whilst Elvis was performing the title song he was called upon to perform an intricate dance routine and he was watched executing this by Gene Kelly,

the Don of the MGM dance musicals of the 1950s. The film was released to the best critical reviews that Elvis had received up to that time and his role earned him the ominous title of 'Mean, Moody and Magnificent', and provided him with a wealth of gold discs to add to his already healthy collection of prize platters.

Following Elvis' debut movie with MGM it was to be another six years before he made another for them, and this was *It Happened At The World's Fair* in 1963. This film, a lightweight musical not too far removed from the kind of films that the studio made in their hey-day, was made in Metrocolour and featured a softer mellower Elvis then the brash unruly youngster of 1957's *Jailhouse Rock*. It was filmed on location at the Seattle World's Fair and gave Elvis's public a chance to see their idol is the flesh, an honour which was to be denied them for a few years to come following completion of his next movie for the company, *Love In Las Vegas*. 1964 saw Elvis complete two movies for MGM, *Love In Las Vegas* and *Kissin' Cousins,* with the latter being released in the USA first, but in Great Britain in its proper chronological order. *Love In Las Vegas* starred Elvis with one of his most electrifying co-stars, Ann-Margaret, and together the dynamic duo produced MGM's most popular musical since *Seven Brides For Seven Brothers,* ten years before. It featured Elvis, quite naturally in Las Vegas, a town he would be closely linked to in the forthcoming few years.

Kissin' Cousins was Elvis' fourth MGM musical and the first of what became known as the 'Elvis-Quickies'. A highly enjoyable movie, it presented the fan with Elvis in a dual role for the first and only time in his movie career, playing a darkhaired Airforce officer and a blonde haired hillbilly. Most fans liked the hillbilly Elvis the best as he was more real, however Elvis detested wearing the wig that the role called for him to wear. 1965 produced two more MGM musicals and these were *Harem Holiday* and *Girl Happy,* the first of which was a terrible attempt at trying to star Elvis in something different, whilst the second was somewhat better, with Elvis playing the leader of a rock combo which featured the son of one of his musical peers (Gary Crosby, son of the late great Bing Crosby).

1966 only produced one Elvis film, however this one was a real winner, its title–*California Holiday*. The film combined Elvis, singing, girl chasing and racing driving, and produced another success along the lines of MGM's earlier hit *Love In Las Vegas*.

European fans got a little excited when they heard that Elvis' next MGM movie, *Double Trouble,* had its screenplay based in London and Brussels. The film however was not shot on location but on MGM's backlot, so the fans' hope

of seeing Elvis on this side of the Atlantic Ocean was but a false one.

Following Elvis' lone MGM film for 1967, he had an exceedingly busy year in 1968 when he appeared in three films for the company, *Speedway, Stay Away Joe* and *Live A Little, Love A Little. Speedway,* the first of the trio promised to be another *Love In Las Vegas,* having as its co-star Nancy Sinatra. The movie however failed to live up to its expectations, but was still eagerly snapped up by the fans. *Stay Away Joe* saw Elvis playing a half-breed North American Indian for the second time in his cinematic career, the first time had been in the 20th Century Fox *Flaming Star.* This new film was a complete departure from the earlier drama in that it was a zany comedy with Elvis playing a role that was quite a departure from anything he had done before. The final movie of 1968 was the ultra-modern *Live A Little, Love A Little,* a slick comedy feature in the old Cary Grant mould. The film failed to get a theatrical release in the U.K. and has only been seen here by courtesy of the film lending libraries and the help of the O.E.P.F.C. and its branch leaders.

From a modern movie Elvis turned to a period piece for his next venture with MGM and this was *The Trouble With Girls (And How To Get Into It).* The film, set in the 1920s, promised to be an exciting movie, but turned out to be little more than a potboiler, with Elvis merely guesting in his own movie. Elvis however looked stunning in his all white attire with trilby and big bushy sideburns, and this made up somewhat for the films shortcomings.

In 1970 Elvis appeared in the first of two documentaries that he would make for MGM, and this was *Elvis—That's The Way It Is,* which turned out to be a block buster of a movie. It gave fans outside the USA their first chance to see Elvis performing live on stage in Las Vegas, and the film became an instant hit with the fans and with non-fans alike.

Elvis' final movie for MGM was made in 1972 and this was *Elvis On Tour,* a film that quite naturally showed Elvis in concert on a tour of mid-America. The film lacked the polish of *Elvis—That's The Way It Is,* but nonetheless it was an important addition to Elvis' list of cinematic achievements, and a fitting epitaph to the output of one of the cinema's most exciting and popular screen idols.

Elvis had one more movie on his MGM contract to complete and this unfortunately was never made due to Elvis being taken from us in August of 1977. One can only hope that MGM can lay their hands on some good unreleased Elvis film material to present to us the fans and the world at large in their final Elvis movie. Let's hope for the best for surely that's what we've come to expect from MGM and Elvis.

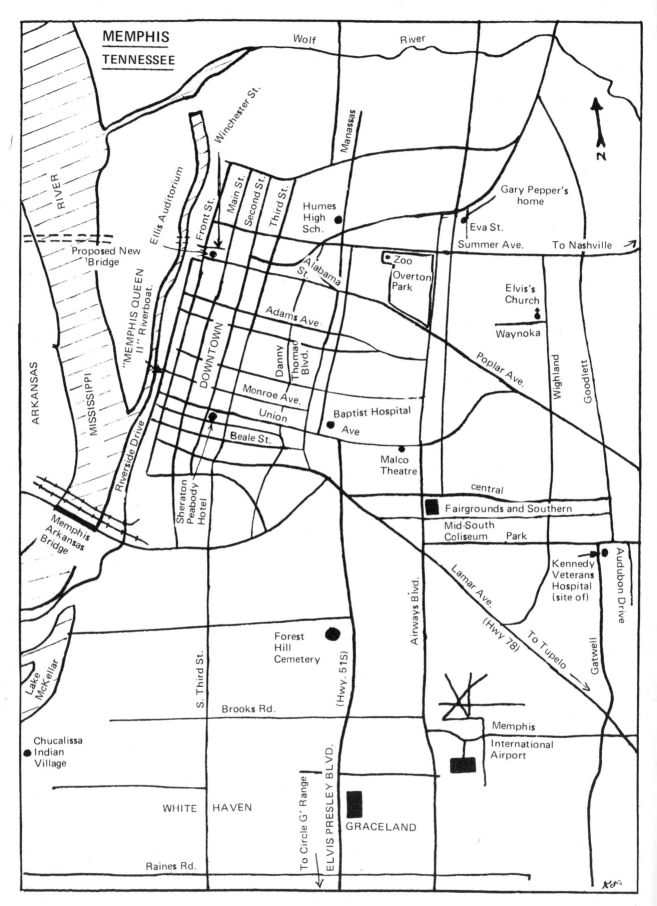

MEMPHIS
TENNESSEE

Wolf River

Winchester St.

Manassas

RIVER

Ellis Auditorium

Gary Pepper's home

Front St.

Main St.
Second St.
Third St.

Humes High Sch.

Eva St.

Summer Ave.

To Nashville

Proposed New Bridge

"MEMPHIS QUEEN II" Riverboat.

Zoo

Overton Park

Elvis's Church

ARKANSAS

MISSISSIPPI

Alabama St.

Adams Ave.

Waynoka

Poplar Ave.

Wighland

Goodlett

DOWNTOWN

Danny Thomad Blvd.

Monroe Ave.

Union

Baptist Hospital Ave

Riverside Drive

Beale St.

Malco Theatre

central

Sheraton Peabody Hotel

Fairgrounds and Southern

Memphis Arkansas Bridge

Mid-South Coliseum   Park

Kennedy Veterans Hospital (site of)

Audubon Drive

Airways Blvd.

Lamar Ave.

(Hwy 78)

To Tupelo

Gatwell

Lake McKellar

S. Third St.

Forest Hill Cemetery

(Hwy. 51S)

Memphis International Airport

Chucalissa Indian Village

Brooks Rd.

To Circle G' Range

ELVIS PRESLEY BLVD.

GRACELAND

WHITE   HAVEN

Raines Rd.

ELVIS COUNTRY
MEMPHIS TENNESSEE

by Anne E. Nixon

Memphis, "a place of good abode", is a city that Elvis fans regard with a special feeling, for Elvis' home is here, and so many places associated with his past and present. Memphis, to which the Presleys moved in 1948, lies on the Mississippi River, and is a prosperous and friendly city. Named by one of its founders, Andrew Jackson, after the Egyptian city of the same name, it still retains some of the charm of the South, while it is a boom town for cotton and industry.

Elvis' home, "Graceland", about 7 miles south of the city, is a major sight-seeing attraction. Not only do Elvis fans worldwide come here, but the Gray Line Bus. Co. makes "Graceland's" famous gates a premium stop on its city tours. Elvis was honoured early in 1972 when Highway 51 South, which runs past "Graceland", was renamed "Elvis Presley Boulevard", and bright green road signs along a 12-mile stretch proclaim this. There's even an Elvis Presley Blvd. Inn, its neon sign looking good at night. "Graceland" has an air of peace and quiet about it, a place of retreat and rest for Elvis. The electronically-controlled wrought-iron gates are guarded, but the friendly guards, especially Elvis' Uncle Vester, let fans go up to the house when Elvis isn't home, and you can have your photo taken lounging in the green armchairs by the front door, or standing on the front porch. Many fans like to visit Forest Hill Cemetery, a mile or two outside the city, on the opposite side of the highway to "Graceland", to see Gladys Presley's grave, and maybe leave some red and white flowers.

Among other places of interest to Elvis fans are his old school, Humes High, located north of the downtown area, and the several homes the Presleys lived in, in this part of the city. The first home was on Poplar Ave., then they were moved to the Lauderdale Courts on Winchester St., and then to Alabama St. Elvis worked at the Crown Electric Co. on Poplar, and Marl Metal Products where he also worked, St. Joseph's Hospital where his mother worked, and United Paint, where his father had a job, are all in this area. Beale Street has several Elvis connections. Lowe's State Cinema was sited here, where Elvis ushered, and Lansky Bros. clothes store is here, where Elvis has shopped often. Beale St. is famous—W. C. Handy wrote the first Blues here —but it's not the safest of streets to walk down. I was told that coloured people outnumber whites in Memphis, and there's a big crime problem. Much of Beale St. is being knocked down, and there are plans to make it into a tourist area. Near the head of Beale St., on Main St., is the "Home of the Blues", record shop, where it's said Elvis has bought many a disc. Next door to the "Home of the Blues" is a photographer's, and I saw photos of Elvis and Priscilla on the walls. These photos appear to date from the mid-60's. Anyone looking for a fine large store is recommended to visit Goldsmiths, along from the "Home of the Blues" on Main St. The staff are friendly, and the store is a fine example of affluent America.

Sam Phillips' "Sun" Recording Studios can be found on Union Ave., and the "Shell" where Elvis made an early appearance, at a C. & W. Jamboree, is in Overton Park. Elvis moved to a nice home on Audubon Drive, after his initial success, and close to Audubon Drive was the site of the Kennedy Veteran's Hospital, where Elvis made an early appearance, as well as being inducted into the U.S. Army from here. Elvis has often rented the Malco Theatre on Union Ave., for all-night film shows, and he used to rent the Fairgrounds at night also. The Mid-South Coliseum, which fans tried to get named for Elvis, is located in the Fairgrounds. Elvis' Church is on Waynoka Road, and in the same area is Eva St., home of Gary Pepper, who was a fine Elvis supporter until the early 1970's, when family circumstances curtailed his activities. Elvis has often been boating on McKellar Lake, and another interest is his ranch, Circle G. The ranch is several miles from Graceland, down the highway and over the Mississippi State Border Line, at Deyes on Horn Lake Road (not shown on the map). In 1961, Elvis made an appearance at the Ellis Auditorium, in a Charity show, and in 1971 the same auditorium was the scene of the Jaycees presentation to Elvis, as one of the Ten Outstanding Young Men of America. Memphis has an extensive Medical Center, and in the Baptist Memorial Hospital in this Center, Lisa was born in 1968, in the Union-East wing. The Methodist Hospital, where Gladys Presley passed away, is on Union Ave., near the Medical Center. Elvis used to give his New Year parties in the Manhattan Club, a mile or so up the highway

from his home, but now uses the Thunderbird Lounge, a private club on the other side of the city. In 1969, Elvis returned to the Memphis studios, and at the American Recording Studios on Danny Thomas Blvd. he cut "From Elvis In Memphis", and others.

There are many other places of interest in the city: Overton Park has a fine Zoo, there is a Chucalissa Indian Village near to McKellar Lake, there are historic homes and museums, and each May Memphis holds a Cotton Carnival— Elvis appeared at the 1956 Carnival. The Mississippi River is a must for a Riverboat ride. The *Memphis Queen II* paddlewheeler departs from the bottom of the bluffs at the foot of Monroe Ave. three times daily in summer, taking you up-river under the beautiful new bridge which is being constructed. A landing is made on a sandbar on the Arkansas side of the river, and from here, you get a fine view of the Memphis skyline. The Sheraton-Peabody Hotel (host to fans on the Destination USA 1972 holiday) has a claim to fame: its ducks. In the fountain in the rather grand lobby there are three or four ducks. At 3 p.m. each day, a red carpet is rolled out, Sousa's "King Cotton March" is played, and the ducks march into the elevator, and go up to their penthouse home!

Memphis-on-the-Mississippi has a lot to offer a visitor, especially if that visitor is an Elvis fan. Memphis, known in Mark Twain's day as the Good Samaritan City because its people gave so much help to persons injured when the Packet Steamers blew their boilers, as often happened. Now, some 100 years later, you'll still find a friendly welcome from most everyone in Memphis, Elvis' home town.

A SPRING VIEW OF ELVIS' MEMPHIS HOME — GRACELAND

ELVIS ★

★ ★ ★

COUNTRY

★ ★ ★

TUPELO, MISSISSIPPI

by Anne E. Nixon

About a hundred miles south-east of Memphis, down the long roller-coaster Highway 78, lies Tupelo, a small but fast-growing city which sits shimmering under the hot Mississippi sun. People in Tupelo have time to stop and exchange a friendly word, and the pace of life is slowed somewhat from that in the larger cities.

For the Elvis fan, Tupelo's main attraction is that Elvis was born on 8th January 1935, in a small wooden shack up the Old Saltillo Road in East Tupelo. Fans from all over the world come to Tupelo to see the birthplace and the Elvis Presley Center nearby. The center has a stage, dance-floor, jukebox, and a framed painting of Elvis on one wall, and in the grounds of this youth facility are a swimming pool, tennis courts, and children's playground, complete with an Elvis Presley Stage Line. The tiny white-painted birthplace has been restored by the East Heights Garden Club, using furnishings similar to those of the late 1930's. It is open daily from 2–5 p.m. —or later if there are a lot of visitors—and attracts around 20,000 visitors a year. In the small backroom is a fireplace, a dresser with cooking utensils, a stove, a table and chairs, and a high chair. The front room has a bed (with potty underneath!), a crib, and a mirrored dressing table. On the walls are rare old Elvis photos and cuttings. The ladies who look after the birthplace are happy to talk with fans, and I was told that Elvis still visits friends in Tupelo; he comes in unannounced and is gone before anyone knows he was there. A white picket fence now surrounds the shack, and shrubs have been planted in the garden.

Tupelo has other places associated with the early Elvis: Berry St., where Gladys' family, the Smiths, lived (Vernon's lived up the Old Saltillo Road); the First Assembly of God Church on Adams St., where Elvis and his family worshipped; the Lawhon school which he attended; the Mississippi/Alabama State Fairgrounds where he sang "Old Shep" at the talent contest so many years ago, and where he made a triumphant return to give a concert on "Elvis Presley Day", 26th September, 1956; the Priceville Cemetery, to the east of the city, where his twin Jesse Garon was buried in an unmarked grave; and the Tupelo National Fish Hatchery south of the Fairgrounds, where his parents often picnicked. Elvis' family also lived on Berry St. and Kelly St., and several Presleys still live in and around Tupelo.

Tupelo has other claims to fame: The Battle of Tupelo was fought here in 1864, and relics of the American Civil War can be seen at the Tupelo National Battlefield Site. The Natchez Trace Parkway passes close by the west of the city, and the Trace Visitor Center is located just north of the city. The Trace was originally an Indian trail, then it became a Frontier trail, used by soldiers and itinerants, to get from Natchez to Nashville. Nowadays, it is a beautiful route to drive along. Cottonfields and sugar cane plantations lie on the outskirts of the city, and pleasant homes line the streets: one-storey white-painted wooden houses, with porches where people laze on sultry summer evenings, and where the fragrance of azaleas, camellias, and dogwood blossoms scents the air in spring. Further out of town I saw wooden shacks amongst the pines, with dark-skinned children playing outside. Tupelo was formerly the capital of the Chickasaw Nation. The name, "Tupelo", is the name the Indians gave to their "Lodging Place", as their homes were constructed from the water-tupelo gum trees. Indian relics are found in the area, and along the Natchez Trace. Tupelo today boasts a fine schools system, and is a centre for both agriculture and industry. It has evolved a much copied Community Development Foundation.

If you ever get the chance, go visit Tupelo, and see where Elvis' roots lie. You will be charmed, as I was, by Tupelo's southern hospitality, and your visit will be a pleasant and memorable experience.

(Thanks are due to Tupelo's long-time Mayor, James Ballard, for his help in connection with the map.)

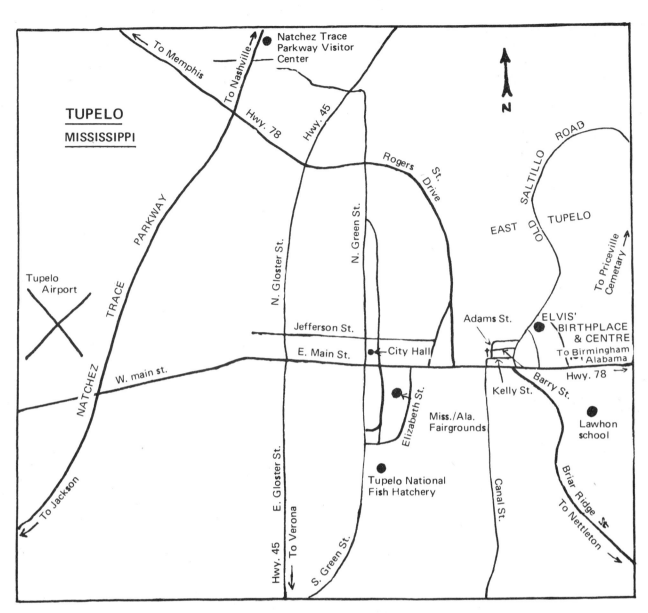

TUPELO

MISSISSIPPI

To Memphis
To Nashville
Natchez Trace
Parkway Visitor
Center
Hwy. 78
Hwy. 45
N
Rogers St. Drive
SALTILLO ROAD
EAST OLD TUPELO
NATCHEZ TRACE PARKWAY
Tupelo
Airport
N. Gloster St.
N. Green St.
To Priceville Cemetary
Jefferson St.
Adams St.
ELVIS'
BIRTHPLACE
& CENTRE
E. Main St.
City Hall
To Birmingham
Alabama
W. main st.
Kelly St.
Barry St.
Hwy. 78
Elizabeth St.
Miss./Ala.
Fairgrounds
Lawhon
school
NATCHEZ
To Jackson
Hwy. 45
E. Gloster St.
To Verona
S. Green St.
Tupelo National
Fish Hatchery
Canal St.
Briar Ridge
To Nettleton

*left: Elvis' Birthplace at
East Tupelo, see map above*

187

FULL LIST OF FILMS COMPLETED starring ELVIS

Love Me Tender 20th Century-Fox
Loving You Paramount
Jailhouse Rock M.G.M.
King Creole Paramount
G.I. Blues Paramount
Flaming Star 20th Century-Fox
Wild in the Country 20th Century-Fox
Blue Hawaii Paramount
Follow that Dream United Artists
Kid Galahad United Artists
Girls! Girls! Girls! Paramount
It Happened at the World's Fair M.G.M.
Fun in Acapulco Paramount
Love in Las Vegas M.G.M.
Kissin' Cousins M.G.M.
Roustabout Paramount
Girl Happy Paramount
Tickle Me United Artists
Harem Holiday M.G.M.
Frankie and Johnny United Artists
Paradise, Hawaiian Style Paramount
California Holiday M.G.M.
Easy Come, Easy Go Paramount
Double Trouble M.G.M.
Clambake United Artists
Speedway M.G.M.
Stay Away Joe M.G.M.
Live A Little, Love A Little M.G.M.
Charro National General Pictures
The Trouble With Girls And How To Get Into It M.G.M.
Change of Habit Universal Pictures
Elvis – That's The Way It Is M.G.M.
Elvis On Tour M.G.M.

Here's a list of some of the King's great, great singles. Some are still available.

Viva Las Vegas/What'd I Say
Kissin' Cousins/It Hurts Me
Such A Night/Never Ending
Blue Christmas/White Christmas
Crying In The Chapel/I Believe In The Man In The Sky
Blue River/Do Not Disturb
Love Letters/Come What May
If Every Day Was Like Xmas/
How Would You Like To Be

Fools Fall in Love/Indescribably Blue
The Love Machine/You Gotta Stop
Long Legged Girl (With Short Dress On)/
That's Someone You'll Never Forget
There's Always Me/Judy
Big Boss Man/You Don't Know Me
Guitar Man/Hi Heel Sneakers
U.S. Male/Stay Away
Your Time Hasn't Come Yet, Baby/Let Yourself Go
You'll Never Walk Alone/We Call On Him
A Little Less Conversation/Almost In Love
If I Can Dream/Memories
In The Ghetto/Any Day Now
Clean Up Your Own Backyard/The Fair's Moving On
Suspicious Minds/You'll Think Of Me
Don't Cry Daddy/Rubberneckin'
Kentucky Rain/My Little Friend
The Wonder Of You/Mama Liked The Roses
I've Lost You/The Next Step Is Love
You Don't Have To Say You Love Me/Patch It Up
There Goes My Everything/
I Really Don't Want To Know
Where Did They Go, Lord/Rags To Riches
Heartbreak Hotel/Hound Dog/Don't Be Cruel
I'm Leaving/Heart of Rome
Jailhouse Rock/Are You Lonesome Tonight/
(Let Me Be Your) Teddy Bear/
Steadfast, Loyal And True
I Just Can't Help Believin'/How The Web Was Woven
We Can Make The Morning/
Until It's Time For You to Go
An American Trilogy/
The First Time Ever I Saw Your Face
Burning Love/It's A Matter Of Time
Separate Ways/Always On My Mind
Polk Salad Annie/See See Rider
Fool/Steamroller Blues
Raised On Rock/For Ol' Times Sake
I've Got A Thing About You Baby/
Take Good Care Of Her
Help Me/If You Talk In Your Sleep
My Boy/Loving Arms
Promised Land/It's Midnight
Suspicion/It's a Long Lonely Highway
Moody Blue/She Thinks I Still Care
Way Down/Pledging My Love
T-r-o-u-b-l-e/Mr Songman

Loving You/Teddy Bear
Gotta Lot o' Livin' To Do/Party
Santa Bring My Baby Back/Santa Claus is Back in Town
Jailhouse Rock/Treat Me Nice
I Beg of You/Don't
Wear My Ring Around Your Neck/
Don'cha Think it's Time
Hard Headed Woman/Don't Ask Me Why
King Creole/Dixiland Rock
All Shook Up/Heartbreak Hotel
Hound Dog/Blue Suede Shoes
One Night/I Got Stung
A Fool Such As I/I Need Your Love Tonight
A Big Hunk of Love/My Wish Came True
Stuck on You/Fame and Fortune
A Mess of Blues/The Girl of My Best Friend
It's Now or Never/Make Me Know It
I Gotta Know/Are You Lonesome Tonight?
Wooden Heart/Tonight is So Right for Love
Surrender/Lonely Man
Wild in the Country/I Feel So Bad
His Latest Flame/Little Sister
Rock-a-Hula Baby/I Can't Help Falling in Love
Good Luck Charm/Anything That's Part of You
She's Not You/Just Tell Her Jim Said Hello
Return to Sender/Where Do You Come From
One Broken Heart for Sale/
They Remind Me Too Much of You
Devil in Disguise/
Please Don't Drag That String Around
Bossa Nova Baby/Witchcraft
Kiss Me Quick/Something Blue